JOHN SADLER & ROSIE SERDIVILLE

ODE TO BULLY BEEF

WWII POETRY THEY DIDN'T LET YOU READ

The History Press

This one is for all of them

Cover illustration: Propaganda cartoon. (U.S. Government Printing Office/Wikimedia Commons)

First published 2014

The History Press
The Mill, Brimscombe Port
Stroud, Gloucestershire, GL5 2QG
www.thehistorypress.co.uk

British Library Cataloguing in Publication Data.
A catalogue record for this book is available from the British Library.

ISBN 978 0 7524 9189 9

Typesetting and origination by The History Press
Printed in Great Britain

CONTENTS

Assist us, O Lord, in these our supplications and keep within Thy protecting hand those who, this night, on sea, land, and in the air, keep vigil on our behalf. Be Thou their comfort in loneliness, their strength in weariness, their defence in danger, and by Thy most gracious and ready help, keep them in all their ways; for the sake of Jesus Christ our Lord.

An Evening Prayer for Sailors, Soldiers, Airmen, Police, Air-raid Wardens, and Firemen

ACKNOWLEDGEMENTS

This book could not have been written without the generous assistance of a number of organisations and individuals. Particular thanks are due to: Roberta Goldwater of *A Soldier's Life* and colleagues at Tyne and Wear Archives and Museums; Ian Martin of the King's Own Scottish Borderers Museum, Berwick upon Tweed; the Trustees of the Green Howards Museum, Richmond; of the Durham Light Infantry Museum and Art Gallery, staff of Durham County Record Office; the staff of Northumberland County Archives at Woodhorn; staff and Trustees of the Fusiliers Museum of Northumberland, Alnwick; colleagues at the North East Centre for Lifelong Learning at the University of Sunderland; staff of the Literary and Philosophical Library, Newcastle; staff of Central Libraries, Newcastle and Gateshead, Clayport Library Durham, Northumberland Libraries at Morpeth, Alnwick, Blyth, Hexham and Cramlington, Lindsay and Colin Durward of Blyth Battery, Blyth, Northumberland; Amy Cameron of National Army Museum; the curator and staff of the Royal Engineers Museum & Archives, Chatham, Captain S. Meadows 2 RGR, Peter Sagar, Kathleen, Wendy and John Shepherd, Margaret Ward, Joan Venables, Ann Havis, Mrs. J. Geddes, David Roberts, editor of the War Poetry Website and Dr. Joan Harvey. Gerry Tomlinson, in particular, has been a source of immense support and stimulation. Special thanks are due to editorial colleagues at The History Press for another successful collaboration.

As ever, the authors remain responsible for all errors and omissions.

Rosie Serdiville, & John Sadler, Northumberland, May 2013

INTRODUCTION

THE POOR BLOODY INFANTRY

Hail, soldier, huddled in the rain,
Hail, soldier, squelching through the mud,
Hail, soldier, sick of dirt and pain,
The sight of death, the smell of blood,
New men, new weapons bear the brunt;
New slogans gild the ancient game:
The infantry are still in front,
And mud and dust are much the same.
Hail, humble footman, poised to fly
Across the west, or any, Wall!
Proud, plodding, peerless P.B.I. –
The foulest, finest, job of all

A.P. Herbert

Poor Bloody Infantry indeed (or P.B.I. as soldiers' slang swiftly had it). Those words have the heartfelt quality of one who had done some marching, although Herbert's military career was actually in the Navy. Unlike many of those whose words appear in this anthology, Herbert would go on to have a career as a professional writer (amongst many other occupations). Heartfelt is the quality that leapt up at us as we explored the archives of the North East, seeking out the reactions of ordinary men and women to the conflict that engulfed the entire world in 1939–45. Sometimes the most prosaic of words summed up a moment or an experience in a way that connected across the decades, and it felt almost as though the writers were speaking to us now.

That opening prayer, for example. It comes from the parish magazine of St Columba's Church at Seaton Burn in Northumberland. Written in October 1941, it conjures up the faces of all those who survived the Blitz and bombing campaigns, all those thinking of men serving away and those at home who had preserved them from harm, 'Their strength in weariness, their defence in danger'. Whoever wrote it knew what it was like to keep watch as the planes came over, night after night. Perhaps it was written by the vicar, Cecil Gault – we don't know for sure because it was unsigned. An ephemeral verse which was not intended for posterity, casual words written to meet a need, to communicate a sense of shared danger, hope and endeavour.

TAINT

'Taint what we have, but what we give
'Taint what we are, but how we live
'Taint what we do, but how we do it
That makes this life worth going through it
Resolve each day to perform what you ought
And to perform without fail what you resolve

J. White (143 Battery Field Artillery)

Much of what appears in this collection is anonymous. Much is doggerel, written by those without any pretension to be great writers of prose or verse. But their words still have the power to reach us from the blank space of their anonymity.

VALE

I am forever haunted by one dread
That I may suddenly be swept away,
Nor have the leave to see you and to say
Goodbye; then this is what I should have said
I have loved summer and the longest day
The leaves of trees, the slumberous film of heat
The bees, the swallows and the waving wheat,
The whistling of mowers in the hay.

I have loved words which left the soul with wings
Words that are windows to eternal things
I have loved souls that to themselves are true
Who cannot stoop and know not how to fear
Yet hold the talisman of pity's tear:
I have loved these because I have loved you.

Anon

1

1939: *SITZKRIEG*

HITLER HAS ONLY GOT ONE BALL
(sung to the tune of 'Colonel Bogey')

Hitler has only got one ball,
Goering's got two but very small,
Himmler is very similar,
And poor old Goebbels' got no balls at all.

Frankfurt has only one beer hall
Stuttgart, die Munchen all on call,
Munich, vee lift up our tunich,
To show vee 'Chermans' have no balls at all.

Anon

It was at 11.00 a.m. on 3 September 1939 that Britain entered a new era. The transition from peace to war was swift and dramatic. The country had put on uniform. No sooner had Chamberlain issued his mournful declaration of war than the National Service (Armed Forces) Act – conscription – came into immediate effect. If there was to be no spectacular rush to the colours this time around, there was at least a steady trickle. Men came forward to enlist voluntarily, more in a spirit of stoical acceptance than in any marked swell of patriotic fervour. It seemed the 'War to end all Wars' had, in fact, changed nothing; a new generation had to pick up the baton. Unlike their fathers, they had few illusions. Sometimes, they leave us with few. These are ordinary human beings, products of their time. Some of their views we can still share, while some jar our modern sensibilities.

BELISHA'S ARMY

We had to join,
We had to join,
We had to join Belisha's army
Fourteen bob a week and FA to eat,
Hob-nailed boots and blisters on your feet
If it wasn't for the war
*We'd have f****d off long ago*
Belisha you're boring …

Anon

Leslie Hore-Belisha was an MP and Minister for War from 1937–40. He was the butt of pronounced anti-Semitism, mocked in doggerel, sung to the tune of 'Onward Christian Soldiers':

Onward Christian Soldiers,
You have nought to fear.
Israel Hore-Belisha
Will lead you from the rear.
Clothed by Monty Burton,
Fed on Lyons pies;
Die for Jewish freedom
As a Briton always dies.

General Montgomery described his famous 'Desert Rats' as a 'citizen army'. Most who served were conscripts, young men drawn from all walks of life who would not otherwise have dreamed of a military career. Theirs was the 'last crusade', the very definition of a 'just' war, fought to remove the tyrant's jackboot from most of Western Europe. Despite this noble purpose, there would be no ecstatic rush to join the colours, no repeat of August 1914:

AND THE BLUE AROUND THEIR CAPS

I must admit my ignorance but just before the war –
I used to meet our Yeomanry, and wonder who they were;
For I'd tumble up against them, of an evening in the street,
Dressed in regulation khaki, but particularly neat;
There were never very many of these horsey-looking chaps;
But I noticed that they wore a strip of blue around their caps.

Now, I'd never cared for uniform of any kind or sort,
And noted Volunteering an unnecessary sport;
Nor could I see a reason why these men should serve the King,
When we had a British Army, just to do that kind of thing.
So, I felt a sort of pity for all Territorial chaps,
With their whips, and spurs, and leggings, or the blue around their caps

But when the war had started, and the troops were mobilised,
I found the parks and school-rooms filled with men I had despised;
They marched along the country roads, and drilled upon 'The Moor'*
And seemed to do a lot of things I'd never seen before;
And if I went to Gosforth in a crowded car, perhaps
I'd meet some "Khaki Johnnies" with the blue around their caps.

* The town moor of Newcastle Upon Tyne

There were lots of other people didn't take to them a bit,
So we'd do a little chaffing, just to exercise our wit,
And talk about 'The Noodles' who were frightened of a horse,
That their drill was simply awful, and their shooting – rather
worse;
But the girls would all declare them quite a decent lot of chaps,
Though they were a bit conceited of the blue around their caps.

'Twas a dull September Sunday, when I saw the Yeomen go,
And I thought the whole procession was a quiet sort of show;
For the people who were watching didn't seem to understand;
There was hardly any cheering and there wasn't any band.
Still, I could not help admiring all those sturdy-looking chaps,
Riding through our ancient city, with the blue around their caps

First, we heard they went to Lyndhurst, which is somewhere in the
South;
Then, a list of idle rumours got about, from mouth to mouth,
Till, suddenly, the newsboys started shouting, near and far;
'Northern Yeomanry in action! Special news about the war!'
It was just about a skirmish and some trivial mishaps;
But it proved that they were fighting for the blue around their caps.

Then I knew that I'd been sleeping, while the Yeomen were awake;
I had simply been 'a slacker' when my country was at stake.
So I joined the gay Commercials, and I did the Swedish drill,
Till I found myself expanding and my chest began to fill;
And when marching with my comrades in the scarlet shoulder-straps,
I could see another meaning in the blue around the caps.

How I wished that – like the Yeomen – we'd been 'ready' from the start;
Fit to meet a sullen foeman, glad to play a soldier's part:
For within that bloody corner of fair Belgium's stricken land,
First of all our Territorials: there to lend a helping hand;
And I ask a humble pardon for uncomplimentary raps
At their swaggering assurance, and the blue around the caps.

Far, amid the deadly shrapnel, they have held the Hun at bay;
They have fought, and fell, and suffered in the trenches of Ypres,
Side by side with gallant comrades from the corners of the earth,
For the honour of the Northland, for the country of their birth,
They have shared in night combats: they have scored in village scraps;
And they've added fame and glory to the blue around the caps!

G. Dodd

We came across this one in the Northumberland Hussars archives. In the accompanying letter (August 1973), Ossie Hall, who had servied in 'B' section and was now on the committee of the Hussar's Old Boys Association, explains that he has reworked the original poem. Hall was sending it on to another Old Boy, Lord Ridley, who would eventually donate it to the Museum. Forty-five years after the start of the Second World War, the marching song of the Hussars still had resonance for this Newcastle man:

MARCHING SONG OF 15/19 HUSSARS

Side by side with gallant commander
From the corners of the earth,
For the honour of the North-land
For the country of their birth
They have shared in mighty combats
They have scored in village scraps
And they've added fame and glory
To the blue around their caps

War was not seen as a great patriotic crusade, more as a chore to be dealt with – an interregnum in the business of living.

Thwaites was an Australian who studied at New College, Oxford before serving in the North Atlantic, finally commanding a corvette. He had an active post-war career, publishing several volumes of poetry. He was one of that rare breed, those who spoke about their war to those close to them.

EPITAPH ON A NEW ARMY

No drums they wished, whose thought were tied
To girls and jobs and mother,
Who rose and drilled and killed and died
Because they saw no other,
Who died without the hero's throb,
And if they trembled, hid it,
Who did not fancy much their job
But thought it best and did it.

Michael Thwaites, November 1939

Many who returned never spoke of their service. It was an episode, necessary but isolated, boxed up in the mind and filed away. A poignant collection of letters from Private (later Lieutenant and then Brevet Captain) Herbert Cook to his future wife Peggy Longthorne, survives in Durham County Record Office. Herbert served in the Pioneer Corps and ROAC in India and latterly Singapore. He was likely a POW but, happily, survived and returned to his Peggy. Their letters are full of everyday events – his plans for promotion, their wedding arrangements, the difficulty of getting out to see your girlfriend when your mam makes her views known.

Bunker, Otto Hirst in *Kunst der Front*. (Courtesy of the Northumberland Hussars Museum)

November 1940

Dear Peggy,

I am very sorry to say that I can't meet you tonight. The reason being that I coughed all last night and the folks say that if I want to go to the dance, I have to stay in tonight ... I was very surprised when mother 'put her foot down' because it is the first time she has done so for years ...

Love, Herbert

February 1941

My darling,

... Coming down here won't cost an awful lot apart from the train fare (soldiers wife's rate) as I can fix you up for practically nothing down here as far as lodgings are concerned, [he appears to be at a Hookswood training camp in Surrey] ... Rations of course, will be quite easy to get from the army, (I have a good pal in the cookhouse here). Plenty of best butters etc. Don't go spending your coupons on me sweetheart, for wool. I think I can do without a pullover until the war is over. If I need one I can wear yours on the days that you haven't got it on ...

All my love and lots of kisses sweetheart,

Herbert.

Thursday

I wonder if we are due any more wedding presents, darling. They still seem to be rolling in ... This is a lousy company for getting 48 hours tacked on to one's leave. The only time it is allowed is

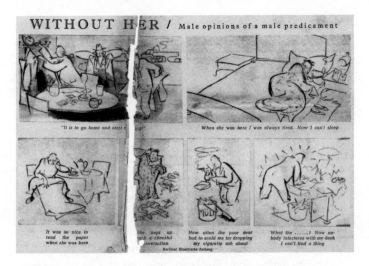

Without Her. (Courtesy of the Northumberland Hussars Museum)

when the railway warrant is made out for Scotland. I think I will have my passant made out for Edinburgh and claim the two days, breaking my journey in Sunderland. Quite easy and no penalties attached.

I am terribly fed up at the moment for news – nothing. The major event prevents me from seeing any correspondence about my commission for locking it in a special file in his safe. Personally, I see absolutely no need at all for all this secrecy. Either it has been granted or it hasn't.

22nd March 1941, Hookwood Camp Surrey

I would have written before this, but I have had a lot of letters to write this week. You see, dear, dad wrote to me saying that he had been talking to a friend of his, a Mr. Davill by name, who lives down here, who says he might be able to get me a commission, and

that he was going to try and see me … So you see, darling, you might
still be able to walk out with a 2nd Lieutenant, (I hope).

April 1941

Darling,

Lt Whiteley came up this lunchtime … he told me that Mr Davill
had been up to headquarters … From what Whiteley said, I got the
impression that Davill had caused a bit of a stir at H.Q. And that
the officers had thought him a hell of a good feller …

From what I hear from chaps coming back from leave, food is very
scarce in 'civvy street' so please don't put yourself out to get things
to send me darling as the food is very good here … Give my love to
your mam and dad.

Love & kisses,

Herbert.

Hookwood Camp, Nr Horsley, Friday

I have just had an interview with Lt Vivian … From what he said,
my commission is going through and he said that the company
officers have pledged themselves to Mr Davill to do all that they
possibly can for me.

At the interview he told me to write another letter, with reference to
my last one, giving alternative regiments to the R.E. You see dear, he
told me that the R.Es were very difficult to get in unless you were
graded A.1. As alternatives, he suggested the Royal Army Ordnance
Corps or the Pioneer Corps. I don't think I will get the 'pips' up for
a while yet as I will first have to be transferred to an O.C.T.U. for

training. However, I shall probably be promoted as an N.C.O. in the near future. So the fortune teller looks as though she is going to be right!

This has put a different complexion on my life altogether darling, as it has given me something else to look forward to (besides the finish of the war). I am now hoping that it doesn't finish before I am a 2nd Lieutenant. However, I don't think that is going to be the case.

I think I will get tight tonight.

All my love, darling

20th March 1942

C/o GPO Bletchingley, Surrey:

I am trying to write this letter amid a terrific cacophony of swing music, and a lot of 'jitterbuggers' revolving round the table. (The accent is on the last part of the word). It's terrible here, as I can't get any decent music on the wireless, with so many swing fans in the billet. I shall have to do something to the wireless in the dead of night.

Peggie to Herbert, full of wedding plans

24th May 1942

I have just come in from Sunderland and believe me dear, I'm fed up. What with the horrible rainy weather and shopping, I wish we were nicely away on our own. I had a reply from Cook's this morning and they fixed us up at 'Willowmere Private Hotel', Waterhead, Ambleside for five days from May 30th. On Tuesday I am going to get the tickets and hotel chit or whatever one calls it and, of course pay the bill … The licence came yesterday so that's a little less to worry about. I got a nice new hat to travel in. I hope you will like it sweetheart … Mum got a new hat too and a very pretty dress …

I was looking for a present for Holly. You know it's the custom to give the bridesmaid one don't you. So far I haven't found anything suitable.

… There's so much to discuss. I rather expect a letter from you this morning; still I hope you've sent one for Monday. I want your opinion so much; I do hope I've arranged things to your satisfaction darling. Lal made me a satin dressing gown as my green one is much too heavy to take away. It looks very nice and the colour is pale green.

I have to do two hours duty tonight to finish my 60 hrs for this week. Next week, thank goodness, I'm on night duty. I'm taking my leave from the Saturday, 6th …

Lots of kisses dear

Peggie xxx

26th May 1942

My Darling,

Gran has given me the wedding ring as she says I would have had it left me in her will & I may as well have it now when I need it: It's 22ct gold & a nice thick one & much better than one can buy now.

I'm glad your Dad has been nice about it. I don't mind how he treats me, as long as he is alright with you … As we haven't got invitations printed, I should like you to ask your relations to the wedding so please don't forget dear. Here's a point we must discuss, as soon as possible, are we to come back to our place and cut the cake & have wine, (we have Sherry and some invalid wine, don't laugh), or do we go straight from the church? You see darling, I can't very well travel in my wedding dress and a hat with lots of veiling flowing behind so I thought if I had time to change into my other things, (my new coat and hat), it would be more sensible. What do you think? If you agree to cut the cake etc, (no wedding breakfast), you should ask your relations to be present; they will then please themselves as to whether they care to come.

I expect you will know by now where we will spend our honeymoon. I'm going into Cook's tomorrow (Tuesday) to get the rail tickets etc. also to find out what time the train leaves, then I must see the vicar about fixing the time of the wedding.

I also want to order flowers and the taxis tomorrow. I think I ought to have two taxis, one for you and your best man & relations, and the other for myself. What do you say to keeping one taxi to take us into Sunderland? I think it's better than bothering about buses.

I can hardly realise it's only three days to go and then I'll see you (for) five days & I'll be your wife and have to get used to being called 'Mrs. Cook'.

I have a lovely story to tell you about fixing things at Cook's Travel agency, you see Herbert, I had to give your name & pay the deposit in your name too, so when I came out, he said 'good morning Mrs. Cook' & I never answered, 'til Gran gave me a knock. I felt such a fool, I'm sure he must have noticed I wasn't used to that name ...

I will see you soon so cheerio, love from No. 4.

All my love and kisses,

Peggie xxx

Hill Croft, Smoke Lane, Reigate, Sunday

My dear Peggie,

I am terribly sorry I have not been able to write sooner than this but we have been out on manoeuvres, prior to the Home Guard affair. Thank God it only poured with rain once that was yesterday ... I have got a bit of a cold through getting wet but otherwise I feel absolutely fit. In fact, I have never felt so well in all my life and I'm more sun burnt than ever. I am, however, covered with gnat bites ...

Well, darling, the last news I have had about leave, is that it has been stopped, from the 28th of this month to the 4th of August, so that I think my leave will be put back a few days. In view of this, darling, I will leave it to you to do what you think best at your end. The point is, dear, that I can't give you any information until the new leave list comes out ...

Love to all at No 4

I am longing to see [sic] darling.

All my love,

Herbert

P.S. Please excuse the writing, as I am lying on my tummy in bed. I am 'wore out'.

(It seems to have all worked out, since further letters are addressed to 'Mrs. H.G. Cook'!)

Bletchingley, Surrey, Saturday evening

Darling,

Or maybe I should begin my letters with 'My Darling Wife'. I think it would sound better. This is the first opportunity that I have had to write but I don't think I shall be able to catch the post this evening.

I had a very uneventful journey back but it was extremely hot and the train was very crowded ...

Excuse the scribble darling as I have forsaken the desk for my bed as it is much cooler in here. And talking about bed, it's a very lonely place now, isn't it, Mrs. Cook? I am absolutely 'browned off' already, darling and the only thing that makes things bearable is the wonderful memory of a few days ago: You and Windermere, the perfect combination.

Everything and everybody down here irritates me to an inordinate degree; the eternal jazz on the wireless, everyone's personal mannerisms and even their little tricks of speech. I am more tolerant of the cuckoos now as they remind me of honeymoons & things ...

Sunday ... It is a pity that the wedding photographs didn't come out very well, but maybe Freda has some better ones. Have you been through to see yet? Which reminds me, darling, why not go ahead and have that 'talk' with Freda, somewhere where there will be no interruptions. Please do, dear, not only for my sake, but for your own, as I don't think it right that you should remain ignorant on these matters, through no fault of your own.

I am going to have a talk with CQMS today about the grounds on which one can get supplementary allowances for one's wife. Nothing may come of it however as you are working and also, I think that most of the allowances apply to those who were married before the war. Nevertheless, I can but try.

Well, darling, I will finish up now as it is almost lunch time.

Give my love to our mam & dad (they are mine now too, aren't they darling). Lots of love to Mrs. H G Cook from her husband Mr. H G Cook.

All my love, darling

Herbert

Wednesday

Darling,

I got your letter with the late post today, one bright spot in an otherwise filthy day. It has poured with rain since this morning & I was feeling absolutely dejected until your letter arrived ...

Nothing ever happens in this place. It's dead. I spend the whole of the day wishing. After about an hour's work in the morning I begin to wish it was time for break at 10.30 am. After that I begin to wish it was lunchtime, and after lunch, I long and wish for tea time. Don't get me wrong, it's not hunger. It's a state of sheer 'browned off ness' which everyone has on returning from leave. And, the whole of the time, I am longing to be with you ...

All my love, sweetheart

Herbert

Same address, Friday

My Dear Peggie,

It's Friday evening, it's raining hard & I am on duty. What a combination. It will be two years tomorrow, by the date, since I lost my liberty and became a soldier. I don't know what you think darling, but it seems more like two hundred years to me ...

Still no news about my commission; I am getting 'browned off'. Something is bound to come through sometime ...

I will have to finish up now darling, as the cook has just come in to tell me my supper is ready. An egg and a large slice of ham, about half an inch thick ...

All my love, sweetheart

Herbert

A soldier's gift – a ladies handkerchief – To My Sweetheart

Monday evening

My Darling,

I was feeling so far down in the dumps on Saturday morning that I asked for the afternoon off and got it. I took the line of least resistance and ended up in the pictures; first time in the pictures for about 4 months. It was a very mediocre affair entitled 'The Courtship of Andy Hardy' or 'Andy Hardy's courtship' or something. It was an appalling bit of extravagance on my part & I have done nothing but regret it (financially) ever since.

As for you possibly being unable to get your holidays when I come home, let me tell you this Mrs. Cook: − if they don't give you leave when I come home, you are going to take it no matter what they say. Every married woman whose husband is in the 'forces' is entitled to leave every time he gets his ... Everything that is said on the subject by whatever authorities you come under will be said personally to me. So, whether you like it or not, Mrs C., you are going to have a holiday in exactly 21 days from now. If I haven't made the position quite clear darling, you had better write and tell me ...

Lots of love and kisses,

Herbert

P.S. Please excuse scribble, as I am lying on my bed and the papers, like me, have no visible means of support.

I WILL COME BACK TO YOU

It was a happy world we shared together, you and I, there were joys and tears, long hours of idleness, and the zest of being young and free. To you I was no hero that day when I became a soldier. Still less was I a hero to myself. It was a war not of my making but in it I have found a cause too precious to betray. This is why one day I WILL COME BACK TO YOU.

Oh yes it might have been easy to have turned aside – I heard no call to battle – only deep down within me a conviction that was greater than myself if I had lived to love you, could I risk death to fight for you? It was a simple echo of the heart that whispers now - I WILL COME BACK TO YOU.

There is only misery in war to those who weigh life in comfort, gold and power. Those are the scales of our enemy and they have called me from your side to challenge our possession of the right to live; men call it 'freedom', but I call it – you. How simple then it seemed as I stand in line, awaiting the order that has already gone forth to thousands of my comrades. Proudly I will press on to victory because I WILL COME BACK TO YOU.

Though out on that battlefield may lie many of those who staked a claim to life, their souls triumphant will go marching on – cleansed by the fire of tribulation in the cause of right. Shoulder to shoulder we will stand – even in death. And if my living comrades of the line should close their ranks for me, I too will be there, content. God's wish will be fulfilled – a night – a little day and I WILL COME BACK TO YOU.

Fusilier McLuckie (RNF)

Britain had 'won' the First World War but what was the face of victory? A whole generation of young men blighted in what seemed, in retrospect, the bickering of a dysfunctional pan-European royal family. The titanic effort expended during the war had to be a one-off. The scale of suffering – the sheer pointlessness of the whole ghastly mess – could have only one conclusion. Such a thing could simply never again occur, it was unthinkable. Britain had never seen centuries of conflict on home soil: unlike the rest of Europe, the marching armies had all trod elsewhere. The shock of a conflict that literally brought war home is hard to imagine.

Yet, when Hitler's pushing the bounds finally overstepped the limits of appeasement and German forces crashed into hapless Poland, Britain and France again found themselves locked into combat.

CASUS BELLI

A sense of moral duty
Drove Britain into War
When Hitler grabbed for booty
The Polish Corridor.
No man of honour doubted
That we were in the right.
When guarantees are flouted,
The guarantor must fight.
For ours is not the quarrel
By fleeting passion stirred
For us the issue moral
Is – that we keep our word

Anon

Young Germans, caught up in the lust for glory saw the rape of Poland in a different light:

GEFREITER

Streams of blood must run over the earth,
The ground trembles, the world shakes;
Where ever de-composing, shot-up heaps
The last men run, hounded by fear
Fire mercilessly strikes the field.

There's drumming and drumming, rumbling and crashing!
The enemy has now got to know us!
For we have provoked this hell,
In which the victor of every battle –
Death – reaps his grim harvest.

Hanns Pfeuffer

Poland fell, crushed whilst the Allies stood by, impotent. Then came the 'phoney war'; gas masks were issued, children were evacuated but war, or the reality of war, still did not come. The British Expeditionary Force (BEF) was deployed. Once again we would fight alongside our French allies. As Harry S. Truman put it, 'If you're not prepared to pay the price of peace, you'd better be prepared to pay the price of war'.

HEROES OF THE DLI (extract)

Up they came from the depths of the mine
From workshop, from office, from school,
They left their homes without a word of repine,
With smiling face and with courage cool
Though hearts might ache, no tear-dimmed eye,
Was seen among the men of the DLI.
With buoyant step and courageous mien,
They passed from our midst one day
As fine a line as ever was seen,
And we gave them a loud hurray,
A ringing cheer – then we said goodbye
To the gallant men of the DLI.

With a clinging kiss and a farewell smile,
Though our hearts were like to break,
As with dread we thought of the long, long while
Of lonely days, filled with ceaseless ache
'The parting is hard', they said with a sigh
The sorrowing wives of the DLI

Let us cheer the homes of the men that lie
By the hand of our foemen slain
To the men who went from our midst to die
On the distant, war-wreathed plain
And remember in love, there are tears and sighs,
In the stricken homes of the DLI's.

Anon

There was heroism, plenty of it. Men and women responded to the call to defend country and freedom, joining the forces or offering themselves as candidates for war work. Some of them had done so the first time round. There is a photograph taken in 1918 where Flight Lieutenant W. B. Wadell and his sister Pat are shown walking through Hyde Park. Both are in uniform, both on crutches. She has lost the lower part of her leg serving as a FANY in France, he is 3in shorter in both limbs, having been shot down at 1,000ft. On the reverse of the picture Pat noted what happened next. He returned to active service with the RAF in 1939. She went back to France to drive an ambulance for the Free Poles and was the only woman evacuated from St Malo.

Perhaps it takes a particular sort of heroism to see the need to play the part whilst remaining realistic about the pitfalls of a military life – the boredom, sometime bureaucracy and disruption of everyday life.

Lisbeth David joined the WRNS in 1942 as a wireless operator and within a year she had been promoted. Commissioned as a third officer, she served with the Cypher office on the staff of NCSO Belfast, then went on to Portsmouth and finally Columbo. She took a master's degree in theology after the war at St Hugh's College, spending the rest of her life in both the private and public sectors.

PORTSMOUTH CYPHER SCHOOL

i think this is hell
i'll say it again
and make my point well
i think this is hell
no doubt you can tell
not prone to complain
i think this is hell
i'll say it again.

Lisbeth David

18-year-old Audrey Lee was from Liverpool. She served in the WAAF from 1941–44 as a flight mechanic and fitter.

ENTRY 118

I sit here,
Gazing around at the faces
Which unmistakably bear the traces
Of utter boredom.
To my right,
Two WAAF's struggle with the timing
Which they are obviously finding
Far beyond their comprehension.
Cpl. Adams,
The best instructor ever,
Is reaching the end of his tether
At our blatant stupidity.
Whilst Ray,
Best brains of the entry,
Deep in thought studies intently,
Fits and clearances.
My mistake,
Ray confesses, with a guilty look,
Displaying the incriminating book,
She too writes verse.

Audrey Lee (Flight Mechanic, E, RAF,
Hednesford, Staffs)

Of course, there were other, even more traditional forms of disruption: that perennial consequence of war:

THEN THERE WAS A SERVANT GIRL

I am a servant girl
I live in Bermondsey
The master and the mistress are very kind to me
Then, one day a sailor came to stay
That was the beginning of my misery
He asked me for a pillow to rest his weary head
He asked me for a candle to light his way to bed
A mere servant girl thought it was no harm
To get in bed with a sailor man
And keep him nice and warm
Early next morning
The sailor he awoke
Went to his pocket, took out a five pound note
Take this me darling
For the damage I have done
I'm leaving you in charge
Of a daughter or a son
If it be a daughter nurse her on your knee
If it be a boy send the bastard out to sea
Bell bottom trousers and shirt of navy blue
Let him climb the rigging
As I have climbed up you.

Anon

2

1940: *BLITZKRIEG*

EDGEHILL FIGHT

Thank Heaven! At last the trumpets peal
Before our strength gives way.
For King or for the Commonweal –
No matter which they say,
The first dry rattle of new-drawn steel
Changes the world today!

Kipling, (written for C.R.L. Fletcher's *A History of*
England, 1911)

UNTITLED

Above the earth, on searchlight-silvered wings, rides death
In his most awful form – the hand of war;
And from the earth in shuddering cry goes up –
Sirens – whistles – bells warn the world
That death rides out with crosses on his wings.

F. Cremer (Sergeant, RAMC, September 1942)

Britain had not been ready for war in 1939. She was marginally less unready in 1940. The 'miracle' of Dunkirk meant costly defeat was not converted into catastrophe: the BEF, bereft of all its equipment, lived to fight another day. Britain now stood alone against the seemingly unstoppable progress of the Nazi juggernaut. Not for the first time, Britain had cause to be glad of that narrow stretch of water, the English Channel, and for the heroism of the RAF which won the hard-fought, close-run battle for the skies over England that September:

(Sung to the tune of 'Land of Hope and Glory')

Land of soap and water,
Hitler's having a bath,
Churchill's looking through the keyhole,
Having a jolly good laugh

Stephen Haggard was a son of empire, born in Guatemala to a diplomatic family. After embarking on a career as an actor, he served in the Intelligence Corps in Cairo, where he knew Olivia Manning. Perhaps he served as the inspiration for one of her characters. He killed himself in 1943 when his married Egyptian lover ended their affair. He was 31 years old.

THE MANTLE

Recruits are issued with dead soldiers' stock;
Field-muddied webbing, brass-work that must mock
Our novice hopes to get it clean.
No tragedy in that: what of the shock
At this first splash of blood I've seen –
This ground sheet that has warmed some dying Jock?
'Royal Scots: Dunkirk'! so reads the rune.
Blood and a name where heroism has been.

This hero's shroud must be my living hide
To shield and warm: Pity is in this pride:
My warmth will never quicken him,
And yet by this he shall be sanctified,
Through blood, and through a bullet's whim;
And the far, uncherished agony he died,
Kindling new life as life grew dim,
Shall lift a new vision above my vision's rim.

Stephen Haggard (Devon, June 1940)

Real fears of invasion were in the air. The Ministry of Information produced a steady stream of suitably upbeat, if rather optimistic, leaflets including 'If the Invader Comes':

> *Remember that if parachutists come down near your house, they will not be feeling at all brave. They will not know where they are, they will have no food, and they will not know where their companions are. They will want you to give them food, means of transport and maps. They will want you to tell them where they have landed, where their comrades are, and where our own soldiers are. The fourth rule therefore is as follows: DO NOT GIVE ANY GERMAN ANYTHING.*

Flight Guard, Eberhard Pfeiffer in Kunst der Front. (Courtesy of the Northumberland Hussars Museum)

PRISONER OF WAR

The Huns had us on the run,
One sunny day last May
We had no ammunition,
So we couldn't stop to play.
They harassed us and chased,
Until we reached the sea
At a little place with tall white cliffs,
That's called St Valery.

They fired on us with all they'd got,
To them it was a lark
They were taught a lesson they'll need one day
In getting off one's mark.
It was the French that led the way
Their dust led to the sea.
If the advance was to be stemmed
'Twas to be done by you and me.

We'd reached the pier and thought so far
That things were going well.
Till Jerry not far behind
Let loose the powers of hell.
Though tired and weary, wet and cold
After so long on the Somme,
Tho' faint with hunger we turned to face
Once more their shell and bomb.

Some took up their positions
At the summit of a hill
And tho' they knew what the end must be
Prepared with right good will.
Each regiment cut up something awful
Some companies, no more than a score,

The rest they left 'neath the Somme's blood stained sod.
And still they went back for more.

The Jerry's outnumbered them ten to one,
The 51st still held fast
If duty meant that they all must die,
They'd stick it to the last.
Of the ships we were told would soon be there,
None ventured in too close.
But we knew they were there
On the horizon clear, some puffs of smoke arose.

Then firing on the German advance
With all that we possibly could
As we were up against tanks, and big 'uns,
We knew we could do no good.
Thick and heavy around us the shells all fell
The dead and wounded too many to number.
Till from our positions
We were at last forced.
Leaving most to their long last slumber

St Valery itself hadn't fared too well.
Like Dante's Inferno it blazed.
Each side of the river, cafes and shops,
Soon to the ground were razed.
As twilight fell 'twas an awesome sight.
Some houses like beacons were burning,
Whilst o'er our heads, that last valiant band ,
Were star lights and Very lights gleaming.

By this time being driven right down to the beach
It was the best we could do, to take up positions:
They soon had machine guns.
We fired all night, never showed any mercy.

Tho' we expected none
From those Huns.
We had first aid posts on the beach,
And the front, cafes, and hotels put to use.
These were shelled too. The Huns with their guns
All humanitarian laws did abuse.

On a three storied cafe, down by the front,
Three consecutive hits did they score.
Yes that was a Red Cross station too.
With wounded laid out on the floor.
Then the word flew round, the boats were in sight.
The boys raised a feeble cheer.
The orderlies started the wound to move.
To take them all down to the pier.

There seemed to be hundreds of wounded.
The fit ones too lined up there.
But still on the beach there were
Thousands who never heard that the boats were near.
It seemed that the elements joined them,
For soon it started to rain
Drenching the wounded,
A fact they did not notice because of their pain.

They'd been there a couple of hours
When an ammo dump near by was hit
All small arms ammunition 'tis true,
But it made those who were there 'sweat' a bit.
It seemed to have been a false rumour.
The ships wouldn't come in that night.
Back to the caves went the wounded.
Back went the fits ones to fight.

Machine guns were placed hors de combat.
Riflemen blown up by the score.
Ne'er has a more bitter tale been told
Than that of St Valery shore.
Meanwhile at the Hospital General,
Which in peace time a convent had been,
Ambulances commenced evacuating the wounded away from the scene.

They took them right down to the sea-front,
Then over the bridge to the right.
On the Dieppe Road, the drivers pulled up.
They were French and so full of fright.
The hum of Hun airplanes fell on their ears.
The wounded that could clambered down
And lay on their faces, not daring to breathe,
As the bombs on their way hurtled down.

Two ambulances there met their doom that night.
The French neither worried or cared.
They'd already 'Packed in' and surrendered at ten.
All the night through they'd been scared.
Their fathers in graves 'neath Flanders Red Fields
Must have stirred in anguish and groaned.
Had they heard now their sons, not soldiers but girls,
Whimpered, grumbled and groaned.

The wounded their own way had to make back.
The drivers too boozy with wine,
They left their ambulances
Refusing to drive them on that road in a straggling line.
The navy on Valery had now opened up.
Under cover of shells they closed.
From the foot of the cliffs our lads ran the gauntlet
'Neath the spattering lead and death.
When they reached the sea, they swam out to the ships.
Traveling with bated breath.

Thus it went on till the red streaks of dawn
Changed the darkness of night to day.
All those on the boat thought the outgoing tide,
Seaward would see them away.
Their hopes were short lived.
From the top of the cliffs big shells started to whine,
Riving great holes in the ship's steel sides.
The soldiers dived into the brine.

As they swam to the shore, disillusionment growing,
The 'cease fire' had already blown.
They came out of the water
With hands raised high, all hope having far away flown.
The Germans were masters that day, it is true.
We were outnumbered in arms and in men.

They took thousands of prisoners,
All of who had quitted themselves like men.
'Twas the bitterest day in the lives of all there,
Who for Britain's honour had stood.
That day in the annals of history will be written in blood.

That was in 1940.
The tables are now turned,
Very soon will come their day of fate,
When our fire on them relentless will fall,
Purging both Nazis and hate.
Then back to sanity, wisdom and peace,
This war weary world will arrive,
And nations as brothers will live the world o'er,
To this end all Britishers strive.

Published by the POW department of the Red Cross &
St Johns War Organisation

Image by Walther Cauer from *Kunst der Front*, a souvenir collected by the Northumberland Hussars from Luftwaffe HQ in Catania, Sicily. (Courtesy of Northumberland Hussars Museum)

After the Dunkirk deliverance, Foreign Secretary Anthony Eden issued his famous call for volunteers. The LDV (soon rebranded as 'Look, Duck and Vanish'), were swiftly replaced by the Home Guard.

ODE TO THE HOME GUARD

Great Britain stood in danger
From the Bully from Berlin
Oh! How the Home Guard was founded
Why it even staggered him.

With prongs and sticks and shotguns
There was John and Joe and Tom
Right through the bally country
The Home Guard was formed and strong.

It helped to save the country
Although some were old and bald
It put the wind up Hitler
For he was heard to say 'Good Lord'.

'Winkle' Ayling (14 May 1943)

Dad's Army contains a great deal of truth: muddling amateurishness, chronic shortages of weapons and equipment, Heath Robinson hardware and the wide divergence of personal backgrounds all strike a factual chord. However, the Home Guard remains affectionately risible because it was never tested. In the event of an actual German invasion, the volunteers of 1940 would have been expected to fight and almost certainly would have done. A memorable scene from the television series features Mainwaring's ill-assorted heroes manning a makeshift barricade, doling out their few shotgun cartridges and awaiting German tanks. The tanks never came; had they done so the results would have been swift, brutal and anything but comic:

> *Tanks are big and strong and bullying in their use, and like most bullies, have some very vulnerable points. Trained tank-hunters, chosen for their courage, coolness and readiness to carry the fight to the enemy, can become such a pest and potential danger to tanks and their crews that the value of both as fighting units can be reduced by more than half.*

> 'Home Guard Manual'

With this rousing if rather vague advice, the warriors of the Home Guard were exhorted to take on panzers. Precisely how they were to strike terror into their armoured foes depended on the use of available weapons. These are listed in the 'Home Guard Manual': 'Hand grenades, issue or homemade, petrol bombs, smoke candles, anti-tank mines, axes and saws, explosives and demolitions, crowbars (for breaking tank tracks) and shotguns (for firing into drivers' and gunners' slits)'. Any Tommy who had fought the same panzers in France might have had some trenchant observations. How you got close enough to ram your 12 bore through the driver's slit was not rehearsed. However, it must be remembered as we laugh that this bunch of amateur warriors were willing to lay down their lives. Documents of the time give the men defending our beaches in the event of invasion a life expectancy of 24 hours.

In December 1940, General O'Connor's Western Desert Force unleashed Operation Compass, an offensive against the Italians which, though successful, heralded three years of desert warfare. The situation was greeted with the usual mix of stoicism and ribaldry:

IF

If you can soldier here without a worry
And eat your bread and cheese and M&V
If when the Stukas come, you never hurry
And bombs and shells and fleas don't worry thee

If you can laugh and sing when guns do rumble
Nor murmur when your tobacco don't last out
If you can eat your stew and never grumble
Yet keep a cheery smile when sergeants shout

If you can hear reveille call each morning
And rise and face the new day with a grin
If you can sleep with fleas about you crawling
And always tell your pal we're going to win.

If you can wait and never get tired of waiting
For mail that never seems to come
If you can face the desert heat each morning
And never let your thoughts stray back to home

If you can play your fiddle as good as Nero
And never swear or curse when things go wrong
Then, all I can say is you're a blinkin' hero
And, what is more, you'll be the only one!

J. Campbell

Desert Santa.
(Courtesy of
Northumberland
Hussars Museum)

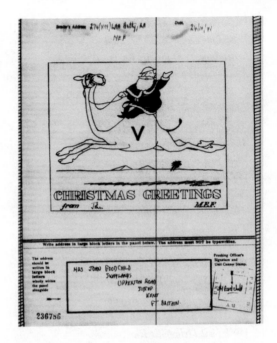

TOBRUK HEROES DREAM

I hear we'll soon be going
To Cairo for a thrill
There to rest our weary bones
And frolic with Tiger Lil
Of course it's just a rumour
So please don't pay much heed
The cook overheard the CO say
Soon to Cairo we'll proceed.

We'll leave behind the ammo
The machine-guns and camouflage net
And in Cairo we will try to find
A blonde or a pretty brunette

We're sick and tired of soldiering
Where the Dago learned to run
Instead we want the city lights
A skirt, some beer and fun.

The cabarets at evening we'll visit
Nightclubs and nightspots we'll hit
And there till four in the morning
With beer and women we'll sit
We'll have the occasional whisky
Perhaps it will be a pink gin
Then dance with a Turk or a Syrian
A French dame or maybe a Finn

We'll visit the Sphinx and Pyramids
The museum and the Egyptian Bazaar
And see the famous dance troupe
That wear nothing but lipstick and straw
We'll visit Heliopolis Racecourse
The ambassadors and ministers met here
Where everyone drinks gin and whisky
Except Tommies, they drink lousy beer.

We'll visit the famous Burka
Where the maidens sit rolling their eyes
Where Tommies and Diggers are sitting
Admiring the figures and thighs
Where every few minutes there enters
Wog vendors, illiterate and crude
Selling watches, peanuts and chocolate
And snapshots of girls in the nude.

J. Campbell

HEROIC TOBRUK
(sung to the tune of 'British Grenadiers')

You may talk of famous sieges of Lucknow and Cawnpore
Of men like Wellington, Nelson and Admiral Rooke
There was Ladysmith, Mafeking and fierce fighting at Lahor
But none to rank as famous as Heroic Tobruk

Blue waters to the north, to the south lie desert sands
Huns and Dagoes whichever way we look
But brave men all and free did leave their native lands
And now they stand defending Heroic Tobruk

Brave youths from Australia and from India's sunny site
From England – and all to their guns have stuck
Daily they are defying Germany's might
The Empire will be proud of Heroic Tobruk.

When all this world is freed from Hitler's boast
And bloody battles are written in a book
Then all free men shall rise and say, 'a toast
To the gallant defenders of Heroic Tobruk'.

J. Campbell

AUSTRALIAN DEMOCRACY

There's a place in the north of Africa
That's bordered by desert and sea
Where many an Aussie has breathed his last
For the sake of democracy

There many a brave hero has spoken
And died that we should remain free
Where Australian youth has fought against odds
For the sake of democracy

Our history books tell us of Flanders
Of Jutland and battles at sea
But by far have the heroes of Aussie
Upheld our democracy

The writer of this comes from England
The heart of an empire that's free
He will always say this, the Australian youth
Are the heroes of democracy.

J. Campbell

MOTHER & SON

There's a silvery haired old lady
Who dreams by the fireside
At a snap she is tenderly gazing
For hours she has silently cried.

She looks at a youth dressed in khaki
Who is barely yet out of his teens
In her eyes there are tears as she whispers
God bless you my boy! Pleasant dreams!

The boy is the pride of her life
But he answered the call like his dad
And so he is serving his country
Whilst his mother is inwardly glad

This curly haired youth barely twenty
Is sweating with rifle and gun
'Neath the heat of a tropical desert
And is tanned by a sweltering sun

Each night he lies dreaming of homeland
As the guns roar and flash overhead
And a silvery haired old lady
Who nightly kneels down by her bed

He thinks of his father before him
Who silently suffered the same
That the honour of England and freedom
Should uphold its beautiful name.

J. Campbell

UNTITLED

Rat-tat-tat-tat you can hear it each night
It's the boys with the old Vickers guns
As they sit in their posts defending Tobruk
All around them is Dagoes and Huns
They have been in the front line for over twelve months
With never a break or a spell
And many a hero of the 'Fighting Fifth'
In combat and battle has fell

Rat-tat-tat-tat, you can hear it each night
As the Vickers guns bubble and boil
The Fighting Fifth's there, well up to the front
The enemy's plans they do spoil
They sit and they grin as the guns spout out lead.
With a rat-tat-tat-tat all night long
The fifth will be there, you never need doubt
With a smile, a shout and a song.

J. Campbell

OLD TOBRUK

Desert, desert everywhere sand and filth and muck
But Freedom's force still stands there, defending old Tobruk
Australians, Indians and British forces
Are there defying Goering's aerial horses

London claims to have had numerous raids, Warsaw and Rotterdam
too,
But in comparison with old Tobruk, they seem mighty few.
Over they come by the score, dropping their loads of hell
But the spirit of that force they never shall repel.

Lord Haw-Haw boasts that Tobruk shall fall
'Good morning rats' is his daily call
We may live like rats in holes dug deep
But freedom's banner aloft we'll keep.

On the sands we eat, on the sands we lie
On the sands we fight, on the sands we die
Defending the last one of freedom's posts
Defying and challenging Hitler's hordes.

J. Campbell

Campbell served in a machine-gun battalion (1st Battalion Royal
Northumberland Fusiliers) 1939–45.

3

1941: STANDING ALONE

During the bombing spree of 1941, North Shields, a port on the Tyne, suffered one of the worst single horrors when a single random bomb from a lone aircraft struck a civilian shelter and killed 107 people. James Robert Ward witnessed the aftermath, searching for the bodies of his family:

The last time I saw Mrs Gibson and Ethel was in the old Wash House on the corner of Church Way and Saville Street, opposite the Alnwick Castle, I was looking at their faces, but they could not look at mine; they were dead, victims of the bombing of Wilkinson's Air Raid Shelter. The Wash House was utilised for a Mortuary. I was in there with my brother Bill, looking for three of our family, they were there with many more we knew.

My Brother Bill and I went through the Wash House, to identify our dead; we managed to get Bill's Wife Lily out and their eldest Daughter Lily. As we went into the Mortuary, the attendant offered us a cigarette, Bill took one, I don't smoke. The attendant had a cigarette case with a lighter attached, the first that I had seen. He could not keep his hands still as he tried to light Bill's cigarette. This man had the worst job in Shields at that moment. Bill steadied his hand and he took us around. The children and small adults were on the top bunks and the big people on the bottom bunks. It was like walking down 'Memory Lane', there was everybody I knew by name or sight, Mr Gibson and Ethel, the Broans from Tyne Street, and one woman in particular, her big black eyes used to make me uncomfortable when I was a kid, and there they were staring at me as before.

I was going to go around the back of the bunks, when the attendant said, 'Don't go around there, there is nothing there for you'. He was wrong. I did go around and found my Sister Lizzie. She had a black eye and I think that she had been pregnant at the time. The back of the shelter was like a Butcher's Shop, all of the corpses were wrapped in Burlap, that kind of Muslin that the Butchers used. Bill had found Ann, Lizzie's Daughter, but could not find Maureen his own Daughter. We climbed up the ladders to examine each child. One did look like her, but the attendant showed me three chalk crosses on the side if the bunk. Three people had identified this child as their own. It was so hard to tell the difference.

AIR RAID

Shrill as a banshee's wail of terror
Low like an oft-heard funeral dirge,
Rising and falling without an error,
Sirens scream – Take Cover – Urge.

Ears attuned to engines droning,
Eyes upturned towards the sky
Children sobbing, voices moaning;
Again, the death from up on high.

Explosions shake familiar buildings,
Dust and debris over all;
Bombs are falling, mangling, killing
Voices for their loved ones call.

Music played by fiends incarnate,
Heard by all with bated breath;
Screams and cries of souls demented
In a symphony of death.

Then, so quickly, comes the silence
Sorrows banish pain and fear
From the shelters voices commence
'There it goes' – Thank God – All Clear.

J.W.

In 1941, 15-year-old Jean Atkinson was living with her family in Newcastle. Her experience of the Blitz is both immediate and personal. Here is a vivid description from a letter of 15 April:

The siren went on Wednesday night at about 12 o'clock and we got up. The barrage was pretty heavy and continuous until about 3.30 a.m., we were so tired that we decided to go to bed. I kept my trousers on (Jack's) and we lay down, we hadn't been in bed more than five minutes when our guns (they're just past the Silver Lonnen) started to go off again. Can you imagine the noise of two 3.7 inch ack-acks going off simultaneously?

Why we stayed in bed I don't know, but we did and, as the planes got nearer I got that horrible cold feeling all over. The guns stopped and the planes seemed to come lower but I never imagined for one moment that they would drop anything because we have often had Jerries overhead and they've never dropped anything. The plane came lower and then I saw a huge flash outside of my window (I don't have a blackout) and then, a big white flash in my room. Something hit the bed, a bit of the ceiling hit my head and I jumped up and as I scrambled out of bed I caught my foot on something red hot. I gave a yell and shouted to ma and pa that there was an incendiary on my bed.

I rushed out and shut my bedroom door. I grabbed my slippers from the dining room because I knew I'd burnt my foot and I ran for the stirrup pump. I was clad in only my pyjamas, trousers, slippers and a woolen shawl. I hesitated on the back step thinking that someone might see me but I forgot my modesty and gave a dash for Watsons where the stirrup pump was. Can you imagine the scene? There were about 30 incendiaries round our street, all blazing, the searchlights, the ack-ack fire and a full moon. It was like daylight or, as mum described it later 'Hell let loose' (excuse language).

I dragged the stirrup pump into the house and, by this time, dad had put half a bucket of sand on the bed. I took the hose into the bedroom while pop pumped the water and mam ran for more water. The whole bed was on fire (for the bomb had landed in the middle of the bed). I knelt down and concentrated the jet on the flames as demonstrated in the films. The smoke was terrible and I had to have a wet rag on my face. This entire time dad had been seeking more sand and mum had been using the pump.

After about five minutes dad took over the hose and I had a little try at the pump. We had the fire out in about ten minutes except for the mattress smoldering. By this time, the whole house was full of choking black smoke and a few men had come to see if everything was alright. Mr. Hare put a burn dressing on my foot and then I went outside and carried a sandbag up to Whittington Grove where there was another fire. When I came back, four men had carried the mattress outside and stopped the smoldering feathers from taking fire.

The 'All-Clear' went at just 5 o'clock; only an hour after the bombs had been dropped. We had a cup of tea and I went to bed (the boys' bed). Mine was wholly gutted, all the bedclothes being ruined. All of my underclothing was burnt because I had them under the eiderdown. On top of this, my dressing-gown which was on the bottom of the bed was burnt. I didn't sleep much because so many people came to view the damage. There was a covering of white dust over everything the next morning, (from the magnesium in the bomb) and it took us a whole day to get rid of the smell in the house but the bedroom still literally 'stinks'!

Jean had four brothers, all of whom saw service during and after the war. She herself became a nurse and finished her career as Head of District Nursing Services for Newcastle West and North.

The Second Battle for the Atlantic was to rage for the entire duration of the war. The first phase (June 1940–February 1941) has been dubbed the 'Happy' time. Happy that is for the wolf packs. The British were reduced to mendacity and begging obsolete 'lease-lend' destroyers from the US whilst U-boats and their 'ace' commanders enjoyed halcyon cruising.

THE PARTY

Three months was the least we would sail,
From Fort St. John to St. Ives,
And we set out again with one hundred-six men
In hopes we would come home alive.

The able on both sides enlisted,
To wage the Great War on their foe,
And the safety of those who were loved and held close
Was the force that compelled them to go.

This was my fourth tour of duty,
With more than our fair share of nubs,
But they would return with the lessons they'd learn,
As long as we stymied the subs.

Two ounces of rum was our issue,
To be drunk before bed for our nerves,
But we stored it away for that most fateful day
No ninety-day wonder deserves.

We checked on our stockpile of foxers*
That were saving our lives by their sound,
Whenever we missed with the DCs we dished,
And the Jerry's torpedoes came round.

* A 'foxer' was an acoustic decoy used to confuse homing torpedoes.

The Third Reich developed a missile
To skim slightly under our wake
And alter its path to deliver its wrath
To the noise the ship's engine would make.

Our Corvette could never stop moving,
For the noise from the foxer would fail,
And the racket that kept us alive would be still
And the 'fish' would be right on our tail.

Rob Walker (written in 2011 from a story told to the
writer by his father who had served on corvettes)

After General O'Connor's successful offensive in the Western Desert which defeated a vastly superior Italian force, Hitler sent Erwin Rommel, soon to become legend as 'the Desert Fox' to shore up Mussolini's disintegrating empire. The Allied position was weakened when Churchill insisted on an ill-starred diversion into Greece. British resources were stretched far too thin; well might the Aussie soldier complain:

RARE AS FAIRIES

We marched and groaned beneath our load,
Whilst Jerry bombed us off the road,
He chased us here, he chased us there,
The bastards chased us everywhere.
And whilst he dropped his load of death,
We cursed the bloody RAF,
And when we heard the wireless news,
When portly Winston aired his views –
The RAF was now in Greece
Fighting hard to win the peace;
We scratched our heads and said 'Pig's arse',
For this to us was just a farce,
For if in Greece the air force be –
Then where the Bloody Hell are we?

Anzac Doggerel

Greece was another debacle, followed by disaster on Crete when German Paratroop General Kurt Student attempted to take the island by 'aerial envelopment' – deploying only airborne troops. Each German paratrooper had, sewn into the lining of his pack, the 'Ten Commandments of the Parachutist'. Both mantra and memorandum, it was a telling mix of sound practical advice and high sentiment:

> *You are the chosen ones of the German army. You will seek combat and train yourselves to endure any manner of test. To you the battle shall be fulfillment.*
>
> *Cultivate true comradeship, for by the aid of your comrades you will conquer or die.*
>
> *Be aware of talking. Be not corruptible. Men act while women chatter. Chatter may bring you to the grave.*
>
> *Be calm and prudent, strong and resolute. Valour and the enthusiasm of an offensive spirit will cause you to prevail in the attack.*
>
> *The most precious thing in the presence of the foe is ammunition. He who shoots uselessly, merely to comfort himself, is a man of straw who merits not the title of a parachutist.*
>
> *Never surrender. To you death or victory must be a point of honour.*
>
> *You can triumph only if your weapons are good. See that you submit yourself to this law – first my weapon and then myself.*
>
> *You must grasp the full purpose of any enterprise, so that if your leader is killed you yourself can fulfill it.*
>
> *Against an open foe fight with chivalry, but to a guerrilla extend no quarter.*
>
> *Keep your eyes wide open. Tune yourself to the topmost pitch. Be as nimble as a greyhound, as tough as leather, as hard as Krupp steel, and so you shall be the German warrior incarnate.*

Put more poetically:

THE PARATROOPS MARCHING SONG

We are few yet our blood is wild,
Dread neither foe nor death
One thing we know – for Germany in need – we care
We fight, we win, we die,
To arms! To arms!
There's no way back, no way back.

German Paratroopers' (*Fallschirmjager*) marching song

Kiwis on the ground met the attack with fierce determination and German casualties were high:

THE SCREAMING JUNKERS

The screaming Junkers over the grey-green trees,
Their cargoes feathering to earth.
They might be wisps of white rose petal
Caught in the keen, compelling twist of fate
Faltering, aimless, in an aimless wind:
Confetti, white and dirty white,
Tossed out in scattered handfuls …

And one man idle leans against the open hatch,
Through which the white horde poured and watches Crete whine
past below,
And in the mixed array of conquest
His hearing does not catch the rifle snap,
Sudden, faint his hands grasp deeply into nothingness,
And in bewildered agony
The dark soul drowns.

He struggles as the troop plane banks;
Un-struggling falls in one slow turn –
The horror dream personified –
And the olives snatch him to their greenery.
Our vague ears do not catch the death – weak cry,
And someone blows the smoke shreds from his rifle mouth.

E.F.U.

The battle hung in the balance before tipping in the Axis favour. The New Zealanders fought magnificently.

FORWARD FOR NEW ZEALAND!

The young hate the old
Yet stumble after them.
Stand for New Zealand!
Yelled Kippenburger,
Country lawyer turned brigade commander
And conveyed ten thousand miles
To practice heroics
On a deadly Cretan hillside.
Stand for New Zealand!
Over the fraudulent field of death
Forward for New Zealand!
You random assembly of farm labourers,
Clerks, roustabouts, shearers, barmen,
Salesmen, commercial travelers, store men,
Mechanics, musterers, drivers, factory hands,
And seasonal workers pressed into temporary khaki …
We are infantry of mettle
Reputed for steadfastness in the attack,
The highest produce of a country that
Breeds men with the animal virtue of blind courage
In the willing service of the herd.
Our lifestyle and instincts instruct us
More cogently than any military precepts.
Forward for New Zealand!

Anon

On 22 June, Hitler's legions stormed across the Russian border; Operation Barbarossa was under way. War to the death in the east had begun. Suddenly Britain and the Soviets, if never truly allies, had found a common foe. In the Western Desert, the 'Pendulum' swung first one way and then the other. This was *Krieg ohne Hass* (war without hate) as Rommel described it, the armies see-sawing over the vast, arid canvas of the sands.

TRIBUTE TO 50TH DIVISION (extract)

Now you've heard of Lord Kitchener,
Long may his memory live,
But when it's soldiers you're needing,
Just send for 50 Div.

When Rommel got to Alamein,
And things were getting stiff
They said 'Britons never shall be slaves',
Then sent for 50 Div.

When things got tough at Mareth,
And very few managed to live,
The highland boys just played their pipes,
So they sent for 50 Div.

And when at Wadi Akarit,
With the 6th on view,
They made a gap and held it
And the Highland Div went through.

They battled to Enfidaville,
Their best they had to give,
They painted HD on the walls,
And sent for 50 Div.

They sent them off to Sicily,
Where they took ridge upon ridge
They even took Lentini,
Then they came to Primosole Bridge.

Our paratroops tried to take it
The Jerry would not give
Which left them just one thing to do,
They sent for 50 Div.

That night they tried to take it
The tears were in their eyes
You could hear their leaders shouting
Come on, the DLI's.

And when at last they crossed it
The ground around was red
With the life-blood of the wounded
And the bodies of the dead.

And they built a monument
At the bridge there in the shade
To the memories of the heroes
Of the 151 Brigade.

Anon

Condor – Georg Reisinger in *Kunst der Front*.
(Courtesy of Northumberland Hussars
Museum)

FORT CAPUZZO

For there will come a day
When the Lord will say – Close order!

One evening breaking a jeep journey at Capuzzo
I noticed a soldier as he entered the cemetery
And stood looking at the grave of a fallen enemy
Then I understood the meaning of the word 'Pietas'
(A word unfamiliar to the newsreel commentator
As well as the pimp, the informer and the traitor)

His thought was like this. Here's another 'Good Jerry'
Poor mucker, just eighteen, must be hard up for manpower
Or else he volunteered, silly bastard, that's the fatal
The-fatal-mistake, never volunteer for anything.
I wonder how he died? Just as well it was him though
And not one of our chaps – yes, the only good Jerry,
As they say, is your sort chum; cheerio you poor bastard.

Don't be late on parade, when the Lord calls 'Close order'
Keep waiting for the angels, keep listening for reveille.

Harry Sanderson (CQMS 1 RNF)

LIBYAN HANDICAP (sung to the tune of 'Blaydon Races')

We were told to go to Libya, one December afternoon
After ice-cream merchants, the fighting fifth did run
Engineers, infantry and Tank Corps chaps as well
Graziani and his crowd, they ran like blinkin' 'ell.

Chorus:
Oh me lads you should have seen us gangin'
Past the Eyeties on the road, with their hands up they were standing
Their officers wore posh uniforms; the rank and file wore rags
But every prisoner we did see was sporting large, white flags.

We flew past Sidi Barrani, the past Capuzzo fort
We stopped outside of Bardia and a battle there was fought
We broke up their defences
And lots of prisoners we did take
Then on the road to old Tobruk with all haste we did make.

Chorus

Tobruk was the next objective, that's what we were told
Supporting Australian infantry went in the old and bold
We made the attack at the crack of dawn
And broke through their front line
Then through the Dagoes we did go, just like a number nine.

Chorus

R.J. Luke (1 RNF)

4

1942: END OF THE BEGINNING

The desert ('the Blue') threw up a whole catalogue of factors to hinder military activity and increase the misery of individual combatants. For these, British and Dominion, German, Italian, French and Greek, it seemed the perfect cauldron of a particular version of hell:

MY THREE STRONGEST RECOLLECTIONS

my three strongest recollections are: the heat, sweat pouring and oozing from me, until I ached and itched with it ... the strange lack of fear ... the seemingly endless hours of utter boredom, observing a low ridge about 2,000 yards away with nothing moving, nothing happening, except the sun beating mercilessly down and one's eyes straining (as I remember our gunner putting it) 'at miles and miles of f*** all'.

British troops were drawn from across the vast, sprawling canvas of empire. Active service in Egypt marked the passing of some 'cushy' billets, places worth mourning:

FAREWELL OUR GALLANT DURHAMS

Tomorrow on the troopship,
Up gangway single file
The DLI are going
To see the glorious Nile.
We mourn your loss in India
And heave a heavy sight
Farewell the gallant Durhams
The splendid DLI.

No more will brass-throats deafen
In the eight-anna stands
The Cooperage remembers
Your prowess for Durand
In quiet Deobali
And on Breash Candy's lawns
From Makin to the Oval
The whole of Bombay mourns.

On every Bombay highway
And betel-studded byway
We'll miss your pleasant faces
In all the cheery places
That you haunt
On buses to Colembar
And strolling down the harbour
At Cyro's and the regal
And the rest.
We'll miss your hearty laughter
But Blighty follows after,
So it's the B.E.S.T

Anon

The land was harsh and gave nothing, showing no mercy to the unwary and punishing all who toiled there. Attempts to make it manageable, to offer some feeling of home, simply emphasised the absurdity of the commonplace. Food for example was bread with sand in it and good old bully beef – perfect subject matter for a Tommy's wit (and pen):

ODE TO BULLY BEEF

You can stew it, you can fry it
But no matter how you try it
Fundamentally it remains the same,
You can hash it, you can slash it,
With potatoes you can mash it,
But when all is done you've only changed the name.

Anon

The British adapted rather better to desert conditions than their Axis enemies. The original Western Desert Force, redesignated the Eighth Army, would become the stuff of legend:

CODE OF THE DESERT SOLDIER

Your chief concern is not to endanger your comrade.

Because of the risk that you may bring him, you do not light fires after sunset.

You do not use his slit trench at any time.

Neither do you park your vehicle near the hole in the ground in which he lives.

You do not borrow from him, and particularly you do not borrow those precious fluids, water and petrol.

You do not give him compass bearings which you have not tested and of which you are not sure.

You do not leave any mess behind that will breed flies.

You do not ask him to convey your messages, your gear or yourself unless it is his job to do so.

You do not drink deeply of any man's bottles, for they may not be replenished. You make sure that he has many before you take his cigarettes.

You do not ask information beyond your job, for idle talk kills men.

You do not grouse unduly, except concerning the folly of your own commanders. This is allowable. You criticise no other man's commanders.

Of those things which you do, the first is to be hospitable and the second is to be courteous ... there is time to be helpful to those who share your adventure. A cup of tea, therefore, is proffered to all comers ...

This code is the sum of fellowship in the desert. It knows no rank or any exception.

Anon

Even the improvised latrines or deceptively branded 'desert flowers' were remembered:

ODE TO A DESERT FLOWER

Of all the Desert Flowers known.
For you no seed is ever sown
Yet you are the one that has most fame,
O Desert Rose – for that's your name.
There's thousands of you scattered around,
O' Desert Rose, some square, some round,
Though different in variety,
At night you're all damned hard to see.

Although you're watered very well
You have a most unfragrant smell;
And just in case you do not know,
O' Desert Rose, you'll never grow.
For you are not a Desert Flower,
Growing wilder every hour;
You're just a bloomin' petrol tin,
Used for doing most things in.

Anon

Private Kenneth Lovell of 'D' Company 16 DLI was one who could vouch for the unexpected hazards offered by the desert rose:

CSM Baker had given me the job of trying to keep down the germs in our rather primitive latrines. To give some sort of privacy some big 80-gallon petrol drums had been laid longwise around their sides. He said, "Get some cans of petrol, pour the petrol in and chuck a match on top. It won't do much but it might keep the germs down!" I did this with a couple of other chaps and we got to the last one. There wasn't much petrol left so I chucked it in, set light to it and sent one of the other chaps to get another can of petrol. When he returned I threw some earth into the pot to smother any remaining flames.

Then, satisfied it was safe; I threw the contents of the can in. There was a hell of a 'WHOOSSHHH!' and a bloody great sheet of flame shot up towards me.

Lovell decided that it was less risky to try and leap through the flames as the wind was fanning them towards him. However, his panicked leap landed him on the slope into the mire and his steel-shod boots afforded no purchase:

Despite all my efforts, I fell back and with a splash landed into the shit! They say the more you stir the more it stinks – I can assure you that's very true!

Happily, the midden proved less damaging than the flames and Lovell's grinning mates hauled him free.

I walked the few hundred yards to the sea and I just laid down in it for about two hours till I was thoroughly cleansed!

The Second Battle of El Alamein opened on 23 October. After a hard-fought, and costly, battle of attrition, Rommel withdrew his survivors. From now on the pendulum would only swing one way and the days of the Axis in North Africa were numbered:

EL ALAMEIN

Then from the place, El Alamein
An empires light shone forth again
Kindled in Sand and the burning sun
And the blood of those whose race was done

Children yet unborn shall tell
How those who fought and those who fell
Placed again in their country's hand
The lump of freedom for their land

Little they thought in a few short years
That their land would be a vale of fears
With infidels in charge and those
Who would not fight the common foes

We who live on, morning noon and night
Must pledge again our lives to re-unite
A nation severed by internal strife
That all may have a new and fuller life.

2nd Lieutenant Murray (*c.* 1948)

ITALIAN MARCHING SONG

Captain, captain of the guard
Summon the buglers all,
Make them stand in the barrack square
And sound the demob call.

Driver, driver of the truck,
Start your engine off,
We're in a hurry to get home;
Of war we've had enough.

Oh driver, driver of the bus,
Run through the streets of Rome;
Make her go like a racing car,
We're hurrying to get home.

Autograph. (Author's collection)

EGYPTIAN FANTASY

He was conscious only of a dull throbbing pain at the back of his head and his mouth and throat were as dry and parched as the desert in which he lay. He did not know how long he had been there, and any attempt at solving the mystery drew a blank.

Attempting to rise, he forced himself up on his elbow. The effort proved too much for his head, which throbbed amidst a shower of coloured lights. He lay back with a groan and tried to think. The more he thought, the more involved he grew, the reason for his condition, his method of arrival, even his location were all rather vague and hazy. He decided to open his eyes. The sudden impact of the sun's hot blinding rays forced him to close them again.

Well, at least he knew it was daylight but why had nobody found him? Was he to be left here to die? The thought of death failed to worry him. It could even be a boon. But to die like this, 3,000 miles from home in a foreign desert ... it was then he heard footsteps. They were definitely footsteps, no hallucination this; getting louder too. He was not to die alone then – maybe not at all.

A drink of water might be all he needed, water! The thought of it increased the burning in his throat. He tried to swallow, he might not be seen! He must call out. The first attempt was a dry croak. The second time, he managed a hoarse whisper – 'who is it?' the footsteps halted; 'It's me, Dasher, and if you want any breakfast you'd better jillo [hurry] or you've had it. Your really should leave that beer alone ...

W.R.N.

Victory had been a long time coming and whilst, as the Prime Minister observed, this was not the beginning of the end, it was clearly an end to the beginning.

EIGHTH ARMY HYMN

O, Lord, our only Master
Our victories were Yours,
Pray keep us now and after
May peace be assured.
Look up you sons of Glory,
The Crusader flags' unfurled;
Remember our true story;
"We fought to free the world".
So hoist our Banner highly,
Our cause shall not be lost;
For we were the proud Eighth Army,
Our emblem was the cross.

Anon

The Architects of the New Europe – postcard collected by Capt. Goodchild. (Courtesy of Northumberland Hussars Museum)

CHRISTMAS AT AGHEILA

Somewhere amid the windswept Libyan sands
In stygian darkness, frozen to the bone,
His great-coat swathed about his limbs,
This Christmas eve a soldier stands alone.

For three years now he has not seen his wife,
Three years of blood and sweat and toil and pain
Three Christmas eves have seen him far from home
Perhaps one day will bring him back again.

For him, no crackers, no comic hats, no party games
No Santa Claus to shake the kiddies hands
No Christmas cards for him, no family feast
His company, the barren empty sands.

As midnight comes, it brings the next on guard
A muttered word, their conversations cease
The corporal, next relief, all three turn around
A star blinks out; it is like a star of peace.

Leslie Davies ('W' Company, 1 RNF)

TANK

Lady of Solitude
and evasions!
Lady of Change, with
a bellyful of nails,
taking your solitary
path through the desert
under naked stars.
Woman whose voice
is the flood of rivers,
with appetite in your
bitter breath –
Say old lady
what bull was it
punctured you
with the seed of death?

Alan Rook

Thirty-four-year-old Alan Rook was a gunner who served in France in 1940 and reached the rank of Major before being invalided out. He later collaborated with the author, Henry Treece.

TO BE A DESERT RAT

If you can keep your kit, when all around you
Are losing theirs and blaming it on you;
If you can scrounge a fag when all refuse you,
But make allowance for their doubtful view;
If you can wait, and not be tired of waiting,
Or, being pushed, let no man push you back,
Or, being detailed, waste no time debating
But force a British grin and hump your pack;
If you can drink, and not make drink your master,
And leave the thinking to your N.C.O.,
If you can meet with dear old Lady Astor
And treat her just as though you didn't know –
If you can bear to see your rations twisted
Into the weird concoction known as stew;
If neither knees nor face are ever blistered,
And neither flies nor fleas can worry you;
If you can face the other fellow's chinnings
And turn deaf ears to their unleashed abuse;
If you can force your heart and nerve and sinew
To serve on guard when you should be relieved,
And swear like hell with all the breath that's in you,
With all the curses ever man conceived;
If you can walk with blondes and keep your virtue,
Or ride in trams and keep your pay book safe;
If needle stabs and castor oil don't hurt you,
And rough angora shirts don't even chafe;
If you can fill a sandbag every minute,
Dream that your trench is Lana Turner's flat –
Yours is the blue my son, and all that's in it.
And what is more, you are a DESERT RAT.

R.F. Marriott

5

1943: BEGINNING
OF THE END

OUR COUNTRY

Our country, which is known to all,
Defender of both large and small.
Her strength is shown in wide-spread lands,
Unvanqished by any clutching hands.

In peace before this scene was set,
Our land was a paradise, never to forget.
With rolling hills, and winding streams,
Home and its comforts, youth and its schemes.

The call to arms cast dreams aside
The war brought havoc both far and wide.
Poland was first, yet how she fought,
But none could stem that Nazi horde.

And now the news is of a different sort,
A fight's a fight not a country bought
Mussolini has led, his empire lost,
Now we'll show Jerry we'll never be bossed.

So here we are Tunisia bound,
The Eighth Army's advancing steadfast and sound.
The shores of North Africa will add to our might,
The end of the battle is already in sight.

And so to you England we send you this sheet,
The thoughts of three men in this desert Fleet Street,
There's a sand storm still blowing, but it's worth it to know,
We'll be back in Old Blighty at the end of the show.

Mohamed Reeves (Sgt G.K.); Abdul Dawson (BDR
G.R.); Mustapha Sowerby (L/BDR J.)

By now four years of war had ensured there were thousands of prisoners, held by both sides. A vast haul of Allied captives had gone 'into the bag' during the Battle for France in 1940 and in the early desert campaigns. Theirs would be a hard and lonely war:

A POW'S MEDITATION

Oh! England think not light of me
That I cherished not thy country lanes
Nor paid due homage to the famed beauty
Of thy most bounteous hills and plains
Spare me your scorn, tho' I was blind
To slender crocus and to daffodil gay
Tho' I gazed aloft with vacant mind
On hawthorn blossom or new mown hay.
For here in distant lands I pause to look
Thro' memory's eye to days of yore
And see, as in the pages of a book
They tender features which I ne'er saw before
In peace never thought I overseas to stray
And though my nature inclines not towards
Grateful am I that fate prepared the way
To know thee England and love thee from afar.

Anon

TO MY WIFE – AN APOLOGY AND A PROMISE

I've not been a very good husband in fact, as husbands go
I seem to have broken all records in giving my wife cause for woe
I used to stop out of an evening, in a club, playing darts with the
boys
And never, at any time, troubled that my wife wasn't sharing my joy
I'd drink and curse, I'd gamble and sometimes I'd rave and shout.
My dinners were left in the saucepan, till most of the taste had
boiled out.
I joined the army against her advice, was stationed a long way from
home,
Had four days leave before going abroad, was captured and no more
could roam.

I wrote to my wife when a prisoner fearing she'd ignore my plea
Requesting that she'd send me quickly some clothes, cigarettes and
beef tea,
Back came the reply as soon as could be full of loving and tender
thought
Saying the goods I required were on their way, with others of various
sorts.
Now, there's one thing captivity has taught me, the worth of my wife
and son
And when I get back to Blighty, I'll see that they join in the fun
They tell me there are model husbands. I don't think they'd call me
that
But if I don't make a better job this time, just call me a 'bloody rat'.

T.R. Cleaver

Prisoner of War Artists

Pinocchio was painted by Warrant Officer Gordon C. G. Hawkins and sent home from Germany as a birthday card for his small son Richard.

Packed and Ready!

A cartoon sent home as a postcard to his wife by Corporal Harold Coulter.

A view seen looking north from an Oflag theatre painted by Major W. F. Anderson.

and

A barbed - wire view painted by Lieutenant Worsley, Official Naval war artist.

'Pooky Rabbit' was crayoned in bright colours for Richard by his father, Warrant Officer Gordon C. G. Hawkins.

A corner of the hospital was the subject of a first attempt at a pen and ink sketch made by Captain Robert Ferguson who has taken up drawing and painting as a winter occupation.

Father to Son. (Courtesy of Northumberland Hussars Museum)

BILL THE BANDSMAN

Ahr Bill he were a right good man
In 'ahr 'ome tahn brass band
He used to laike a long trombone
By gum it sahnded grand.
He 'ad a uniform an all
All done i' red and gold
It's in a glass case now at 'ome
Be'in saved for when he's old.
There's moth balls in all t' pockets
There's patches in the pants
He 'ad a new dress suit an' all
He kept that at his Aunts.
I remember once we 'ad a do.
He laiked i't local park.
He didn't need no music
He were used wi playing i't dark
He often were misunderstood
When laikin there wi't lads.
He often 'ad to turn and say
Now stop it off you cads.
One day the bandstand were on fire
All t' flames shootin 'igh
Bill played till t' local fire brigade arrived.
His solo 'T' firefly.'
But t'worst occourance that cam rahned
Were wot he did wi't' slide
He didn't notice t' park soperintendant
Were standin by his side,
As t'Super stepped i'front of him
To fill Bill's glass wi' beer

Bill pushed 'is slide wi' all 'is might,
It went dahn ti' Supers ear.
Bill pushed and shoved and sucked, and blowed
T' conductor missed it all
Until t' trombone were called upon
But T' Super 'ad it all.
The music stopped, all lent a hand
To pull it from 'is lug.
'Ahr Bill were that there worried.
He supped all t' beer i't jug
And when it were suggested
That t' Super should be took
Away i't' bus to t' hospital
Bill were badly shook.
'An what will I do like,' he asked

J.D. Sharp (from *The Clarion*, vol. 16, Sept/Oct 1944.
Produced in Stalag 244, Germany)

UNTITLED

You've got to be witty to know what they say
In our bachelor city, way down Lamsdorf way,
We're all ranks and stations, but pick of the best,
And our limitations can still stand the test.
We've a lingo unbeaten by Esperanto
Our methods of greeting just wait, and I'll show.

There's 'wotcha old Tosher' and 'Oppo, 'ows tricks?
They say 'Howoy cosher?' or 'Bungho, old brick?
Some Scotsman are 'Haggis' but most prefer 'Jock'.
Whatever the tag is, it sticks to a bloke.

There are 'Owd swede basher' and 'Pompey' and 'Raff',
And 'Tankie' and 'Smasheer' and 'Paddy' and 'Taff'.
Of course there is 'Lofty' and 'Busty', and 'Tich'
And 'Happy' and 'Softy' – it's hard to tell which.

There's 'Lankey' and 'Yorky' and 'Geordie' and 'Butch'
And 'Slim' – very gawky – who'd break at a touch.
There's 'Darky' and 'Soapy' and 'Dusty' and 'Snow',
There's 'Bluey' and 'Nobby' and millions more – oh!

You'll find 'Dhobi-wallash' and 'Diggers' and 'Bocks';
'Suckers' with dollars, and 'Cahucks' with smokes.
You've got to be clever, or you're sure to stray
In our bachelor city way down Lamsdorf way.

P. Brooks (*c.* 1941)

The Penny-a-Week Fund was set up by the Red cross and St John's Ambulance Joint War Organisation (JWO) to fur Red Cross parcels for POWs and soldiers serving overseas. Sponsored by the TUC and employers' groups, workers would have a penny a week deducted from their pay and sent directly to the JWO. The sum sounds insignificant, but bear in mind that the average wage at that time was £10 per week. By November 1939 the fund was raising £6,000 a month. As the war progressed, more and more people became involved. The total donated was £17,663,225 – almost £2.5 billion by today's values

Five young tracers from the Surveyors Department of Powell Duffryn Limited, Ystrad Mynach, Glamorgan sent in this poem with a donation to the Penny-a-Week Fund:

THE PRISONER OF WAR

Accept this, our donation for the Prisoners of War,
Made by the sale of calendars and Xmas cards galore.
We are but five young tracers and we've made our own design
And printed all by hand a thousand cards without a whine.
Individually each card is made, no copying, no stencil.
A box of paints, a brush, a drawing pen and just a pencil.
Altho' the work entailed has used up nearly all our leisure,
We wish to state emphatically it's been the greatest pleasure
And tho' we've sometimes floundered when we're making up our rhyme,
Each card has its appropriate verse and is dispatched in time.
So to conclude, we send to you the best of Xmas cheer
And may the boys look forward to a happier New Year.

1. Re-enactor Bill Pickard. (Courtesy of Gilmar Ribeiro, Time Travel Northumberland, Woodhorn)

2. The perfect re-enactor's car. (Courtesy of Graham Trueman)

A story has been told in court that a man tried to persuade his wife to get a divorce by offering her a bottle of whisky. Very few men could afford a divorce and a bottle of whisky at the same time

3. Divorce Second World War style – from 'The Camp',
December 1943. (Courtesy of Northumberland Hussars Museum)

4. 'More Fuel Now', by J. Gaffron. (Author's own collection)

5. 'Up and At Am!', Yates Wilson. (Author's own collection)

6. Ladies silk Handkerchief with the regimental motto 'We Shall Be Worthy'. (Courtesy of Northumberland Hussars Museum)

7. The remains of war. (Courtesy OF Graham Trueman)

8. Wartime defences. (Courtesy of Adam Barr)

9. 'Dig for Plenty', by an unknown artist.

10. A land army girl and horse drawn plough, by Laura Yates,
c. 1944.

In the West, Italians and Germans were driven out of North Africa, followed by an Allied invasion of Sicily. It was the first major blow directed against the Axis heartlands after victory in North Africa and formed a curtain-raiser for the subsequent invasion of the Italian mainland, hammering nails into Il Duce's political coffin and heralding the demise of his regime.

War being what it is, there were times when there was little cheer on offer. One task dreaded by every officer was sending the letters to bereaved families. Painful enough in itself, it must have felt even worse when Tommy's relatives replied. However, perhaps there was also some comfort there for the officer, as the replies make it clear how much the personal contact meant.

Captain John H. Goodchild was 45. A Londoner by birth and a reservist with the Field Artillery, he served with the Northumberland Hussars, winning the MC in 1942. Amongst the items he left to the Hussars' archive was a collection of letters he had received from grieving families.

18 April 1943: Mr. A. W. Fisher, of 52 Nuns Moor Road, Newcastle upon Tyne to Lt Goodchild:

Dear Mr. Goodchild,

I very much appreciate your kindness in sending us your letter of 28th March [Alf was killed on 22 March 1943] which was the first intimation we received about the death of our Alf. It certainly broke the shock we would have received on receipt of the War Office telegram.

His mother and I are deeply grateful to you for your sympathy which we will always appreciate.

Perhaps when you get a little time, you will let us know where he was killed and also where he is buried. I think you will understand, Sir, that any little thing in connection with his death, that you can let us have, will be greatly appreciated by his mother and I.

Will you please also thank Sgt Nichols for photographing his grave and if you can let us have these, we shall be very grateful

Again thanking you for your kindness believe me,

Yours sincerely,

A. W. Fisher

Nichols's photograph of Gunner Fisher's grave at Enfidaville. (Courtesy of Northumberland Hussars Museum)

Mrs. I. Norcup, from 44 Slaney Street, Newcastle under Lyme wrote to John Goodchild on 16 August 1943:

Dear Sir,

Thanks very much for your kind letter concerning my son Arthur BDR [bombardier] Norcup. It was a great shock to me as he was my youngest and we only buried his dad a short while ago. My son wrote and told me that he had got a small parcel for me and I would like you to see if you could do anything for me if you would (it was a table cloth, I believe).

I remain yours,

Mrs. Norcup

P.S. If a parcel should arrive please share it with his pals. The parcel was sent on Aug. 5th '43

Gunner Alf Fisher. (Courtesy of Northumberland Hussars Museum)

On 22 April 1943 Mr. James Galloway, 56 Larkspur Terrace, Jesmond, Newcastle upon Tyne had written:

Dear Sir,

We received your letter dated 28/3/43 [same date as the one to the Fishers] four days before War Office notified us. Your letter gave us a shock that we will never get over. Jimmy was our only lad. We lived for his coming back and his mother built castles in the air. He came in the last war and died in this, mebees [Geordie for maybe] it was all meant to be.

We thank you for this letter from you, it is well put together, a beautiful letter and will always be in our keeping … I trust that you will come safely through and will you come to visit us.

Again thanking you,

James Galloway

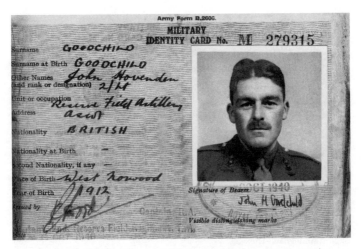

Captain John Goodchild. (Courtesy of Northumberland Hussars Museum)

Mrs. Turner, of 42 Chester Road, Seven Kings, Ilford, Essex wrote on 2 May:

Dear Mr. Goodchild,

It is with my greatest appreciation I write to thank you for writing to me on ... the death of my husband. It came to me as a terrible blow as I had not received any news about him. I had received official news 9 days after receiving your letter ...

I cannot realize that my little girl or I will never see my dear husband again. I dare not stop to think of the future ... what lies ahead of us as my little girl has suffered ill health ever since she was born so of course it makes it a great deal harder for me.

I do not know if you can help me as regards my husband's personal belongings as I should very much like to have them if you could do anything about sending them on to me and I will forward postage to you. I am sorry I cannot write any more as words fail me for the loss of my husband has been a terrible blow for we have had many ups and downs during our few years of married life owing to losing our little boy, ill health of my husband and unemployment and we have pulled together hoping to see our little girl grow up but the Lord knew it best to take my husband away from all this sorrow and strife. So I must say thank you very much for all the trouble you have gone to in writing to me ...

Yours sincerely,

Mrs. B Turner

Pain and loss, fear and uncertainty: they were part of everyday life for those in the services and those on the home front. Mothers would watch their children leave for school in the morning with no certainty of their return. Many women would be off to carry out war work in some form or another; thousands of them joined up themselves.

Everyone agreed that, of the women's services, the WRNS clearly had the smartest uniforms:

THE TALE OF TRANSPORT

First of the bunch we have Mary
No longer a mere leading-Wren,
But, with gold buttons catching the sunlight,
She now holds the rank of chief Wren.

Her surname no longer is Chapman,
For she married the pilot called Bill,
But he's fighting the war on the ocean,
So she's able to be with us still.

Next there's the PO, yes Dodo,
Whose dimples are still in full view,
And there are many who cannot resist them
Now, you, sir! – I ask you, could you?

She is now the Admiral's driver,
And really does look very smart
In a duffle-coat specially dyed navy –
That coat is the joy of her heart!

Cynthia has been promoted
And now on her sleeve wears a 'hook'
Which it took her a full week to sew on,
You can see it's well done if you look.

Her Robin is still out in Egypt,
But to her he's forever The One.
Though she flashes her eyes at Canadians,
We all know it's only in fun.

Anon (1943)

For the first time Britain experienced a mass influx from across the Atlantic as American servicemen poured into the country; 'Overpaid, oversexed and over here' was the phrase:

THE SCOTTISH GIRL'S LAMENT

Dear old Scotland is not the same;
We dreaded invasion, well it came
But though it's not the beastly Hun
The god-damned Yankee navy's come.

You should see them in the tram and bus
There isn't room for both of us.
We walk to let them have our seats,
Then get run over by their jeeps!

You should see them try to dance
The grab a partner, start to prance;
When you're half-dead they stop and smile
Say 'How ya doin', honey-chile'.

Alas, they have not fought the Hun,
No glorious battles have they won.
That row of medals just denotes,
They crossed the sea, brave men in boats.

And they'll leave you broken-hearted;
The camp has moved, your love departed.
You'll wait for mail which will never come,
Beginning to realise, you're awful dumb.

In a different town, in a different place
To a different girl with a different face,
'I love you dear, please be mine',
The same old Yank, the same old line.

Freddy

Let's hope that particular Scottish Girl had not already given her promise to one of the men serving in the Italian campaign!

To the men who spent two long and terrible years slogging up the deadly spine of what proved a very inhospitable peninsula, Italy was anything but visitor-friendly. Many who served there felt they were another forgotten army after June 1944, playing second fiddle to the main event in North West Europe.

Lt E. Yates served with 16th Battalion Durham Light Infantry, firstly in North Africa then in Italy. He was killed in action in October 1943. Aside from a body of correspondence he left the following poems, worthy of any wartime anthology:

PARADE SERVICE ON DECK

'Greater love hath no man',
We turned our eyes away
To where the sunshine on the hills
Claimed glory for the day.

'Than this that he should give',
Our thoughts cast far away
To red-gold hair, soft creamy skin
And sunlight in the bay.

'Should give for his friend his life',
Our memories floated wide
And wandered in some distant vale
To the lapping of the tide.

'Amen', the chaplain's voice soft fell
We bowed our heads to pray,
'Oh God, it cannot be, this price
So soon be ours to pay'.

E. Yates

BEACH CASUALTY

He lived, before the baleful sun
Was risen to burn the yellow sand
To which from out the seas he ran
And then, a moment later, died.
His voice, as stumbling through the surf
He shouldered friends in the khaki wave,
Was mix't with theirs, as strong and rough,
And then, no call or moan he gave,
He laughed, it mingled strangely with a sigh
His thoughts we knew, were far away
And lonely, as the sightless eyes
That saw no beauty in the bay.
Yes, lonely and quiet, as the single grave
Shallow dug beyond the clean washed sand
Safe from the curl of the grasping wave
He lies, and has passed the barren land

E. Yates

ITALIAN PHRASES

Where can we fill our water bottles?
Dove petramo riempire d'acqua I nostril otri?
Doh-vay peh-traym-moh ree-aym
Pee-cay dank-wah ee noh-stree oh-tree?

Where does he live?
Dove abita?
Ay poh-tah-bee-lay lakh-kwah?

E. Yates

SALERNO FRAGMENT

Along the twisting terraces of broken view
The silent colonnades, the shattered arch
Look down on dust-masked things that pass
Tired, waving shadows in the ghostly streets,
Stumbling in rubble spewed from gaping mouths
New torn in tall, smooth walls, cool-drenched
I' the moon, up-stretched to the violent sky
Night blue with layering patterns of fire overlaid
Cool scent of sage in the scrub, with acrid fumes
From roaring, vicious flames, mix in the nostrils
And darkening, climbing pillars of dust
Mask from the cool, smooth sea and the plain
The placid farms and ominous, towering hills.

E. Yates

An accompanying note from the poet reads; 'this poem perhaps delayed in topicality by the time it reaches you may, I hope have achieved its attempt to capture the mood and pictures of the subject'. He died a few days later.

THESE ARE YOUR SONS

These are your sons –
These from the Tees, the Wear and the Tyne
These splendid, eager youths who own
Nothing so great as stands
Before the need of labour from these hands
To wrest the mailed power from those who hate,
All that they are.

These are your sons –
Those who late on Durham fell and moor
Gave of their best as they gave themselves,
Freely, with courage
And the bright example of the young in age
Who were not called, yet strained the leash
That now is slip't.

These are your sons –
Coal, steel and iron have tinged their blood
Fresh, bright blood now mingling with scarred veins
Bringing new strong vigour
And young, gay laughter to the northward pour
Of armies where the Elder and the Younger sons
Are side by side.

These are your sons –
These youths that are now midst the tide
That laps, breaks, tears the bastion of the Hun
A tide of Faithful men
Exalted by sword, oft honoured by the pen
Yet satisfied if cause be just and sacrifice
Be not in vain

These are your sons –
But – these too were sons
Of whom the poet said 'We will remember'
Before we learned and laughed with bitterness
At infidelity
And found it our fault that such should be.
Think hard, remember and bear well this charge
It shall not be
Again

E. Yates

Listening duties, Julius Herburger in *Kunst der Front*.
(Courtesy of Northumberland Hussars Museum)

George Fraser Gallie (1922–2006), served in the Royal Engineers through north Africa and Italy – this poem was written in 1943 when he was 21.

A VOYAGER'S SONG

I drove through the desert of dusty tracks
Through many a Sicilian street.
Past acres of vineyards and orchards and flax
And mile after mile of red poppies and wheat.

I drove past the Sphinx and the Cairo zoo,
And remembered the trips that I used to do.
And I thought of my friends
And I thought of 'Craig Mor'
And the old Austin 10
And the hut on the shore.

I lay on the sands of Syracuse
in the heat of a Mediterranean noon
I nakedly swam in the crystal hues
Of the silvery sea by the August moon.

I dived in the foam of the breaking wave
And remembered the spots where I used to bathe.
And I thought of my friends
And I thought of 'Craig Mor'
Of the rattling stones
And the hut on the shore.

I sauntered down the rutted track
Which wound its way past white-washed farms,
I felt the sun on my naked back
The Italian sun on my face and arms,

I smoked my pipe as I went my way
And remembered the pleasures of yesterday.
And I thought of my friends
And the hut on the shore,
And I thought of 'Craig Malin'
'Cregneish' and 'Craig Mor'

George Fraser Gallie

After June 1944, public attention switched to the decisive battle in Normandy and north-western Europe. The men still battling up the peninsula found themselves a largely forgotten army:

D-DAY DODGERS (sung to the tune of 'Lili Marlene')

We are the D-Day dodgers out here in Italy,
Always drinking vino, always on the spree,
Eighth army skivvies and the Yanks,
We live in Rome and stuff our pants,
We are the D-Day dodgers out here in Italy.

We landed at Salerno, a holiday with pay,
Jerry sent the band to cheer us on our way,
He showed us the sights and gave us tea
We all sang songs and the beer was free
We are the D-Day dodgers out here in Italy.

Naples and Cassino were taken in our stride
We didn't go to fight there; we just went for the ride,
Anzio and Sangro were just the same,
We did nothing there to prove our fame,
For we are the D-Day dodgers out here in Italy.

On the way to Florence, we had a lovely time,
They ran a bus to Amalfi – through the Gothic Line,
Soon to Bologna we will go
When jerry pulls back beyond the Po,
For we are the D-Day dodgers out here in Italy.

Now Lady Astor please listen to this lot,
Don't stand on the platform and talk a lot of rot,
You're such a sweetheart, the nation's pride,
But your damned mouth is far too wide,
That's from the D-Day dodgers out here in Italy.

If you look around the mountains, in the mud and rain,
You'll see a lot of crosses, some that bear no name,
Health, wreck and toil and suffering,
The boys beneath shall never sing,
That they were D-Day dodgers out here in Italy

Anon

6

1944–45: THE
SECOND FRONT

EISENHOWER'S ORDER OF THE DAY

Soldiers, Sailors and Airmen of the Allied Expeditionary Force! You are about to embark upon the Great Crusade, toward which we have striven these many months. The eyes of the world are upon you. The hopes and prayers of liberty-loving people everywhere march with you. In company with our brave Allies and brothers-in-arms on other Fronts, you will bring about the destruction of the German war machine, the elimination of Nazi tyranny over the oppressed peoples of Europe, and security for ourselves in a free world.

All of Amsterdam, all of Holland, in fact the entire western coast of Europe all the way down to Spain, are talking about the invasion day and night, debating, making bets and – hoping.

Anne Frank (diary entry, 22 May 1944)

Operation Overlord heralded the long-awaited opening of the Second Front; the Allies' grand assault on Hitler's 'Fortress Europe'. A vast armada of ships and scores of aircraft moved a mighty army. The battle for Normandy, which both sides knew must be decisive, raged until mid-August.

THE LEGEND OF BILL MILLIN – D-DAY PIPER

The sighing surf on sand abounds, and seabirds call, the only sounds
At break of summers day, and yet, within the hour men will have met
Their destiny as war's shrill chatter ends this tranquil scene. The clatter
Of machine guns spit their hate, as landing craft nose in to grate
Against the shingle to disgorge their human load who wait to charge
Into oncoming deathly hail, but never faltering, nerves taut, pale
Faced, leaping down into the cold wet breakers, seeking firm foothold.

Struggling forward, arms raised clear to gain refuge ahead, so near
And yet seeming so far away as spiteful guns traverse and spray
The killing ground that lies ahead, already littered with the dead
And dying who would never see this bitter, bloody victory.
Then faintly, through the deafening din, an alien sound is heard, the thin
Melodious wailing cry of highland pipes, though bullets fly
Around him, he is unscathed still. Thus starts the tale of Piper Bill.

Bill, who piped for Brigadier Lord Lovat, raised a special cheer
When, leaving on the previous day, took up his pipes, began to play
"Road to the Isles", as, leaving Hamble river for this costly gamble,
Lifting spirits of the men, calling, cheered and cheered again,
Who as the Solent slipped away, all knew that on the following day
They'd face their own worst fears and doubts, prayed that when it came about
They would stand firm and conquer fear to face the perils that appeared.

And now, amid the smoke and roar of high explosives, Bill endures
The hail of death, which all around leaves him untouched, while yet the sound
Of 'Highland Laddie' fills the air as fingers on the chanter dare
To still defy the lethal storm, this awesome hell in all its forms.
Yet death and wholesale demolition, backdrop to this exhibition
Of the art of Scottish piping, even with the bullets sniping,
Will not quiet this hardy Scot, surviving mortar shell and shot.

He marches at the waters edge, still playing, able still to dredge
From deep within his mortal soul the courage to maintain and hold
Himself upright despite the urge to run for safety, then emerge
When all is still and quiet again, escape the trauma and the pain.
But Bill is made of sterner stuff, clutching his pipes he starts to puff
And fill the bag, then with a squeeze, his hands again with practiced ease
Launch into yet another air, lifting spirits everywhere.

And so the legend now is born, as Bill continues to perform
Beyond this strip of golden sand known as Sword Beach, where many men
Have fallen, sacrificed their all in answering their country's call,
But in this page of history this part of France will always be
Where Highland Bagpipes did their part with inspiration, and gave heart
To all who witnessed Bill that day, who, when he crossed that beach to play,
With all his great panache and poise, gave the Highland Pipes their voice.

Tony Church

The events of 1939–45 still have the power to move us: a generation which has never known a conflict on such a scale remains fascinated and involved. Every year thousands of historical re-enactors recreate the 1940s – hoping to keep alive our consciousness of what was done for us.

Sometimes, it's more than just a recreation of the period, as seen in the wedding picture; the bride, groom and guests all wear the clothing of the period. Their reception may have been less austere but it showed all the style and ingenuity of the era. 'The Legend of Bill Millin' is another bow to a previous age. It was written in 2011 after Lord Lovat's piper, whose actions on D-Day became the stuff of legend, had died the year before.

Re-enactors' wedding, 2007. (Courtesy of David Stonehouse)

One of those who came ashore on the Calvados coast was Maurice Pinkney who, after pre-war service with the Durham Militia, enlisted in the 7th Green Howards in July 1939. Maurice was to see much hard fighting, firstly in North Africa and then with 50th Division on Gold Beach. His experiences are recorded, in part at least, in verse.

ON THE WAY

In an English bay at peace we lay, on the second day in June,
And to fore and aft, there are thousands of craft. We'll be heading to
France pretty soon.

The heart and soul of movement control lay in getting us down to
the shore.
And the organisation and administration is better than ever before.
Here a naval Rover, our welfare takes over. He gives us our loading
orders,
While up in the sky the RAF boys fly high and guard us from Jerry's
marauders.
The troops are on board. Our vehicles are stored, and the captain
yells "Anchors aweigh".

Somewhere in France (Author's own collection)

Then gently we slide with the outgoing tide, to take up our place in the bay.
Our orders we know. We wait the word, 'Go' then the world's biggest battle begins.
It will not be in vain. France must live again, and the Nazis must pay for their sins.

Maurice Pinkney (June 1944)

Though the cause was just, Maurice was not a great admirer of the sea or at least not of crossings in crowded troopships:

A SOLDIER'S CRIBB

Who longs for the sea? I can tell you, not me,
My experience has not just begun.
I've done many trips on various ships.
As a soldier it isn't much fun.

Now a sailor be frank, on landing ship tank,
As far as the Tommy's concerned,
Things are a bit flat. You'll agree about that.
And I'll swear something better we've earned.

As a typical sample, take this for example.
More than five hundred troops are on board.
The proverbial cat – no room to swing that.
You can't say one lives like a lord.

The accommodation and bed situation
Is six to one bed, 'tis quite true.
And the food that they serve isn't fit for a pig.
No wonder the sailors wear blue.

At the signal for rally we dash to the galley
For biscuits and bully-beef stew,
Diced carrots and spuds, with a dash of soap suds,
And cold tea from yesterday's brew.

The next meal we get, the coffee is wet.
Our spirits are too but why worry.
We oft' wait for hours in hail, wind and showers.
But what of it. We ain't in no hurry.

The NAAFI – there's none, ship's library – no bon.
There isn't a book in the place.
Understand why I'm blue. There's nothing to do.
I'd sleep but I can't find a space.

But we'll probably grumble when onshore we stumble,
And wish we could move in reverse.
For we're landing in France and there's every chance
That conditions there will be worse.

The going is tough but we're made of the stuff
Of which all British soldiers are made of.
Though we grumble and rile in true British style,
There's not a damned thing we're afraid of.

So let's get at the Hun, Let's get the war won,
And let's get back to our loved ones at home.
Forget about war, have peace evermore,
So that never again need we roam.

Maurice Pinkney

Like most soldiers, Maurice was not reflecting on grand strategy. His thoughts were with Mary, his future wife who was at that point serving as a nurse:

LOOKING BACK

My heart is still in Winchester though I left there long ago.
I can still see the trees as they sway in the breeze, and the river so graceful and slow.
I can picture the blossoms blooming as I stroll in the cool twilight,
Inhaling perfume of the lilac in bloom and the scent of the flowers so bright.

There is also another attraction, a girl by the name of Mary.
She is lovely, attractive and twenty, and graceful as any fairy.
In a sheltered spot on the rolling downs we would sit and admire the view,
While deep in the woods a thrush would sing and the cuckoo would chant his 'cuckoo'.

Yes I saw it in sunny springtime, the happiest time of the year
When mating birds build their nests for two and romance was in the air.
But I'm sure had I seen it in autumn or under a cloak white as pearl
I would love it. If I could but stay there, stay always with Mary, my girl.

Maurice Pinkney (June 1944)

France proved less congenial. Maurice recorded his experience of Normandy for his local newspaper, The Northern Echo, in 1994 for the 50th anniversary:

I felt it was an honour going back to France that day. Apart from the excitement I can't honestly say what our thoughts were that murky morning. Everything seemed to be such a mix up yet order was automatic. Getting ashore was not so difficult, as it seemed Jerry was caught on the hop. The most anxious part was getting off the beach up a steep incline. We had to get forward, because there were thousands of people behind us – jostling and shoving like a football crowd. Once the defending forces got over the initial shock, they threw everything they had at the Allies, while thousands of Royal navy shells screamed overhead in reply. I felt very vulnerable. It seemed that every bit of shrapnel, every bullet, every hand grenade or mine was meant for me. Being in a Bren gun carrier, I did at least have an inch of steel around me. The hardest part of any adventure of this kind was seeing a pal knocked over and not being able to help. One was drilled not to stop but let others following up deal with the casualties.

Maurice, tactfully for one who was courting a nurse, found time to pen an ode praising their contribution:

SALUTE OUR NURSES

Folks say, 'Salute our Soldiers' who battle in the war.
They do not seek for glory but peace for evermore.

Why not, 'Salute our Nurses', now that we are well,
Who nursed our tortured bodies back from a living hell?

Let us speak in admiration of their mercy, faith and love.
Pray then in your heart of hearts, 'God bless them from above'.

This is just the humble thanks of a soldier once in your care.
I forever will remember to salute our nurses everywhere.

Maurice Pinkney (July 1944)

Maurice came safely home and married Mary. He died in December 2003.

One who had cause to remember his 21st birthday in August, as the battle for Normandy reached its denouement with the near annihilation of German forces meshed into the Falaise Pocket, was W.R. 'Nobby' Noblett serving with the 15/19th Hussars:

I WILL ALWAYS REMEMBER MY 21ST BIRTHDAY

The task of 'R' Squadron 15/19th was to support the [43rd] Division across the seine at Vernon while Recce Squadron were given the task of finding an un-blown bridge across by one of those many villages which bordered the river. Anything less like a Recce would be unimaginable. The road towards the villages on our side of the river was totally exposed to the opposite bank. As we had no cover whatsoever we made a s**t or bust dash down the cart track of a road, a tactic we were to employ time and again. The first village we came to – 'bridge blown', as was the next and then, bingo, we found one intact. I don't' know who decided it but a newly-appointed lance-corporal by the name of Alquist was volunteered to go over the bridge first, a decidedly risky operation in view of the fact it was almost certainly ready to be blown.

After many attempts at trying to put our hero at his ease, he and his driver slowly mounted the ramp in their Daimler Scout Car and 'Boo-oom' up went the bridge in a cloud of splinters. I think the calmest person of all, who took it in his stride, was lance-corporal Alquist. On the evening of the 27th [August], we crossed a bailey bridge at Vernon, put across by the divisional engineers. Because the bridge was under enemy observation and artillery fire we did another Formula One gallop. At dusk we pulled up in a line [of scout and armoured cars] by the side of a road covered by a hedge. We laid up there until the morning – according to Ken Butler's diary, it rained all night.

I was awakened next morning by Lieutenant Neville Fellows with the words – 'come on Nobby, wake up and Happy Birthday, your mother's sent you a cake and it's your turn for guard duty!' it was my 21st birthday and it was a beautiful summer's morning as we advanced in line up the road. The tanks had passed us sometime during the night and were now engaging the enemy further up the road. They had received some sporadic fire from the field on our right, just off the road. There was no intelligence as to the strength of the enemy so Recce was ordered forward to suss the place out. It was hard to picture a more peaceful scene than a harvested cornfield with the corn stacked in stooks all over the field.

We advanced about 500 yards off the road onto the edge of the field – all quiet then, suddenly, we came under rifle and MG fire. I saw Ozzy Spanton charging down one side of the field to our right, throwing hand grenades with great abandon, a sight to see. Suddenly, there was silence then, three enemy infantry appeared with a white flag. It was all so innocuous, like watching a film in the cinema.

I remember thinking that wasn't very hard. I saw Captain Bill Robb climb down out of his Humber Scout Car, (a vehicle I never liked, it could not reverse fast enough for my liking), to accept the surrender. Then, all hell broke loose, the whole field erupted with enemy small arms and he was severely wounded. Lieutenant Dickie jumped out to help. Bill Robb, died of his wounds, 'Slapper' Drake and Tommy Dakin were also killed. Everyone was firing back at the enemy who could not be seen, they were dug in behind the corn stooks. So we withdrew to regroup. Ken Butler was to lead us from now on. The lesson to be learnt – this was an operation totally unsuitable for our resources. The Colonel sent tanks in to set fires and destroy the field. We rounded up and took 200 prisoners. My last memory was of Ben Johnson shepherding a shocked group of prisoners by shoving them forward with his scout car.

I will always remember my 21st Birthday …

Memories of Northumberland.

During the years of occupation, resistance to the invader had taken on some quixotic guises:

Mon Colonel,

At Lannoy, chief administrative point of the counties comprising the north and the smallest town of France, the 5th Northumberland Fusiliers Regiment, accompanied by their band, had established their HQ in May 1940 at the Chateau of Prevost, belonging to Mr. Requillart. The German attack in Belgium witnessed the departure of the regiment and their leaving with me, on the spot, a small number of men to guard the material and the musical instruments belonging to the regiment.

Following the hasty retreat, the robbery and stealing of May 1940, the arrival of the Germans at Lannoy, then the occupation of the chateau by these savages, as they were – the first Nazis broke up or destroyed all the materials of every kind, going so far as to put their bayonets through the drum. It is this drum that I, Maurice Wanin, manager and tenant of the Hotel de Vie, Café du Lannoy, was charged to look after. I had taken it into the chateau with the intention of hiding it from these brutes. I hid it very carefully until Liberation Day. I informed three British officers who were visiting our district who, in turn, informed the officer commanding their regiment.

This was, Mon Colonel, the story of the drum.

Please accept, Colonel, from an old solider of the war of 1914 – 1918, the assurance of my sincerity and respect …

M. Wanin.

After further adventures and bureaucratic meddling, the drum was re-united with the Fusiliers and returned safe home.

❖ ❖ ❖

A souvenir of France sent to his wife by Cpl. L Payne. (Courtesy of Northumberland Hussars Museum)

Following the heady days of liberation; the celebrations of Paris and Brussels, the Allied offensive began to stall. Operation Market Garden, Montgomery's attempt to outflank the Siegfried Line and thrust into the belly of the Ruhr, proved disastrously a bridge too far. In autumn mud the Americans stalled whilst the Germans gathered their reserves for one last great effort, *Wacht am Rhein* – the Battle of the Bulge. They were stopped but the war went on.

7

EMPIRE OF THE SUN

KOHIMA

When you go home
Tell them of us and say
For your tomorrow
We gave our today

War Memorial inscription, Garrison Hill

Since Japan's surprise attack on Pearl Harbor on 7 December 1941, British and Imperial forces had been waging a savage and unrelenting war, initially in Malaya and Burma. These campaigns had begun disastrously. Singapore had fallen in shame and humiliation. Burma had been overrun. This war was fought in a deeply alien land, harsh, remote and hostile:

CALL OF THE WEST

I'm sick of the Chinks and the tartar, I'm sick of the Japs and the Malay,
And far away spots on the chart are no place for a soldier to stay.

I've had enough under-sized chicken, and milk that comes out of cans,
The East is no region to stick in, for this particular man.

I'm weary of curry and rice; all co-mingled with highly spiced dope,
I'm weary of bathing in Lysol, and washing with Lifebuoy's soap.

I'm tired of itch-skin diseases, mosquitoes and vermin and flies,
I'm fed up with tropical breezes, and sunshine that dazzles the eye.

To eat without fear of infection, to sleep without using a net,
And throw away all my collection of iodine, quinine etc.

To join in the mesh and clamour, the hurry and the feel of the West,
I trade all the orient glamour that colourful bards would suggest.

Oh Lord for a wind with a tingle, an atmosphere zestful and keen,
Oh Lord, what a pleasure to mingle, with crowds that are white and clean.

They talk of the East as enthralling, that's why I started to roam,
But now the old homestead is calling, oh Lord, how I want to go home!

Anon

Buoyed by seemingly easy victories, the Japanese developed a casual contempt for their British and Indian adversaries, a complacency that would become a dangerous limitation:

SOLDIERS

In my dreams
I see them marching
Into Marathon
Bloody, indomitable
To save the civilized world
I see the Old Guard
Marching through the snow
Indomitable in defeat
In my dream I weep.

And then they materialize at Waterloo
Marching with steadfast discipline
Into the bayonets of the British Square
Each unconquerable, each immortal.

My dream changes
To a dusty road on the Bangkok Plain
I am surprised these are coolies
A rabble, demoralized beaten
Down each leg runs a bloody stream.

I see a tall figure at the head of this column
A wraith like figure who reminds me of Moses
I am wrong, he is a soldier
He gives the word of command.
March to attention the 5th
I see a metamorphosis

I was wrong, they are soldiers
Indomitable in defeat as in victory
That gives eyes right to the Jap
Guard room with a conscious arrogance
And sink to the ground on the Padang
Exhausted but undefeated
The Padang has become strangely English
After this we loved Colonel Flower
I stir in my sleep and dry my tears.

Henry Howard

Recovery was initially slow. Led by General William ('Bill') Slim, the Fourteenth or 'Forgotten' Army had first stopped the Japanese dead in the pivotal battles of Imphal and Kohima and had then swept them clear out of Burma.

Fighting was murderous, no quarter asked or given, and frequently hand-to-hand:

At the next bunker, a Japanese soldier rushed out. He knew if he stayed there he was going to get a grenade in, so he came out of the back door, which was behind me. I didn't see him when he fired. He got me through the side of my face. It felt like being hit by a clenched fist but it didn't hurt as much as a really good punch in a fight. I spat out a handful of teeth, spun round and he was a few paces away, facing me. He had a rifle and bayonet. I pressed the trigger but I'd got no ammunition. As he came towards me I felt it was either him or me. I was an instructor in unarmed combat, so I let him come and threw the light machine-gun in his face … Before he hit the ground I had my hand round his windpipe and I literally tried to tear it out. It wouldn't come − if I could have got his windpipe out I would have twisted it round his neck. We were tossing over on the ground. I managed to get his bayonet off his rifle and finished him with that.

DEAD JAPANESE

Why does your pointing finger accuse,
your black arm, swollen (skin stretched tight
as a surgeon's glove) point, accuse?
Was your cause just
that you accuse me, your enemy?
You the aggressor, I the defender?

Why do you stink so, fouling the air, the grass,
the stagnant pool in the creek?
No other animal stinks so in putrefaction.
Why do you vent your protest against life itself?
Is it seemly for the dead to fight?

Have you not known the sun,
the sweet softness of a woman's breasts,
rest after work?

Then let your arm drop to your side, as in deep sleep;
hasten your decay, sink into the earth,
unloosing your last hold on personality
to know, unknowing, every man's rebirth
in other life; so, when the winds pass, you may be
part of the sweetness of the rippling kunai grass

Charles McCausland

McCausland was an Australian. He served in the infantry, first in the Middle East and latterly New Guinea where this poem was written in 1943. After the war he became a teacher and academic.

WRAP UP ALL MY CARE AND WOE (Sung to the tune of 'Bye-Bye Blackbird')

Wrap up all my care and woe,
Here I go swinging low,
Bye-bye Shanghai!
Won't somebody wait for me,
Please get in a state for me
Bye-bye Shanghai!
Up before the colonel in the morning,
He have me a rocket and a warning:
'You've been out with Sun-Yat-Sen,
You won't go out with him again',
Shanghai, bye-bye!

Anon

Then, at last it was over, there was leave and homecoming:

LIAP 22B

The clerk cried out, 'your LIAP's due*
That long, long journey across the blue
To the land of rations, coupons too,
'Will you accept it?' Too bloomin' true!

The Customs are keen, one pal says,
They'll look you over as far as your shoe,
Nothing escapes them – you've had it chum!
Are you still going – too bloomin true!

Another shouts, I've just come back.
You can't get fags – and beer's short too.
But there's plenty of rain, of that there's no lack
But all we can say is – too bloomin' true!

We all have tried our hardest, it's plain to see
To give you the picture of the land of the Few,
Do we wish you 'good luck', 'bon voyage', 'safe return?'
Do we? Of course – too bloomin' true!

J.L.

*'LIAP' stands for 'Leave in Addition to Python'. This cryptic
description refers to the Python scheme, which from 1944 guaranteed
home leave to those who'd served for four years and more. LIAP was an
additional furlough which kicked in after two years and nine months.

On leave, Karl Staudinger in *Kunst der Front*. (Courtesy of Northumberland Hussars Museum)

8

AFTERMATH

RECESSIONAL

God of our fathers, known of old –
Lord of our far-flung battle line –
Beneath whose awful hand we hold
Dominion over palm and pine –
Lord God of Hosts, be with us yet,
Lest we forget – lest we forget!

The tumult and the shouting dies –
The Captains and the Kings depart ...

Rudyard Kipling

Martin Southall was a Brummie who served as a platoon commander in Italy with the Queen's Royal Regiment. After the war he worked as an engineer, contributing to a number of publications.

AFTERMATH

The battle was long over.
Clothed in hospital blue
with white shirt, red tie,
he was wheeled across
to face a full-length mirror.

Silently
he took in the trouser-legs
pinned back to just above
knee level.

Jacket sleeves treated
in like manner,
folded back through
one hundred and eighty degrees.
Again, pinned neat,
Bristol fashion.

'You'd think,' he said,
Glancing at the mirror-imaged nurse,
'You'd think that, with a name like Cassidy,
they'd have left me just one
sodding leg!'

Martin Southall

In 1918, after the guns had fallen silent, Lloyd George had promised returning veterans 'a land fit for heroes'. It was a noble sentiment but the reality proved very different. Their sons were more cynical and there was a feeling that things had to change. Disillusion with the prevailing order was widespread.

Lieutenant Robert Osborne Hutton of 2 RNF edited a short unpublished pamphlet of verse, 'I Want to Go Home'. This is not necessarily entirely comfortable reading but reflects a strain of bitterness which was current at the time.

These people who are beating the drums of war in our newspapers are not the same who rush out of trenches at the head of their units when assaults are being made … The soldier at the front talks differently. He is seeing things as they are. He knows that this war is the rich man's war and the poor man's fight. He knows that the profiteers, politicians and Jews are heaping up money while he is stuck in the mud … He does not want that those who remained at home should take away his job, that the rich idlers should turn away his girl, that the magnates of industry should build new palaces with his bones. He does not want it! He wants to go home and put things right there.

I WANT TO GO HOME

I want to go home.
Machine-guns they rattle, the cannon they roar;
I don't want to go to the front any more.
O! My! I'm too young to die!
I just want to go home.

Anon

WHAT ARE WE FIGHTING FOR?

To free the world from iron chains,
To help our brethren nigh and far,
Or to increase a rich man's gains,
Are they the reasons for this war?

To gain our freedom, was it lost?
Or capture more renown?
To render aid, no matter cost,
And asking thus, no curtains drawn;
What are we fighting for?

Was England's freedom blighted?
Or did we stand alone?
Or were we too far sighted,
With an eye to every throne?

We know now what a war can do,
To make up for years of peace;
And knowing this, the chosen few
Provoked a fight that will not cease,
What did they do it for?

No answer can the fighter give,
Just a tool, no more, no less,
To die or, perchance, to live;
There's only God can guess
What we are fighting for.

Anon

MEDITERRANEAN SONG

There's some who say the Medi-
Terranean Air is heady;
While others, who have stayed there
Are very much afraid there's
A lot more to be said
About the highly vaunted Med.

For instance there's malaria
In the Mare Nostrum area;
And pox, in many a guise
Small and cow and otherwise
Can easily be caught
Doing things you didn't ought.

Then there's flies and fleas and
Lice and crabs, that tease and
Make themselves a pest
Always hanging around the test-
Icles; playing hide and seek
In the ballroom, so to speak.

And many more afflictions
That cause a lot of restrictions;
The brothers 'dyer' and 'gunner'
Are active winter and summer.
And dysentery's a damned in-
Convenience notwithstanding

So I think that you'll agree,
That those who say the sea
Is nearly always blue,
(Which is nearly always true)
Are deliberately misleading
The folks who judge by reading
That the Med for sure and certain
Is the place to do some flirting.

But you and I know better,
And you can bet an old French letter -
Box, that when this war is over
I'll count myself in clover
As long as I've a bed,
And am nowhere near the Med.

Anon

WHEN THIS BLOODY WAR IS OVER

When this bloody war is over
O! How happy I should be
When this bloody war is over
No more church parades on Sunday.
No more asking for a pass
Tell the bloody Sergeant-Major
To stick the passes up his ...

Anon

HAS ANYONE SEEN THE COLONEL

O! Has anyone seen the Colonel?
I know where he is! I know where he is!
I know where he is!
Has anyone seen the Colonel?
I know where he is!
He's dining with the Brigadier

Chorus:
I saw him! I saw him!
Dining with the Brigadier,
I saw him dining with the Brigadier.

Has anyone seen the Major?
He's down in the deep dug-out.

Has anyone seen the Captain?
He's away on six weeks leave.

Has anyone seen the Subaltern?
He's out on a night-patrol.

Has anyone seen the Sergeant?
He's drinking up the Privates' rum

Has anyone seen the Corporal?
He's hanging on the old barbed wire.

Has anyone seen the Private?
He's holding up the whole damn line.

Anon

HAPPINESS LOST

Whenever I think of happiness
Appears your face, in it I see
A host of love and gentleness
And fond, sweet thoughts of me.
I look towards a future black
Darkened by some jobber's wish,
But happy memories take me back
To you, your smile, your kiss.
Ever in my thoughts will be
The happiness we've known,
Enjoyed in perfect harmony,
They call it home, sweet home.

Anon

STAND BY YOUR GLASSES STEADY

O! Stand by your glasses steady
Though this world be a world full of lies.
And we'll drink to the dead already,
And hurrah for the next man who dies.
Betrayed by the country that bore us;
Betrayed by the land that we love,
Now so many have gone before us,
And they live in the skies up above
Beneath these low hung rafters
Lie the ghosts of the lads that we love,
And at home
Live the bloody old bastards
Responsible for this war that we loathe.

Anon

LONESOME FOR MY DAD

I'm lonesome for my daddy
Since he has gone to war,
To fight for some man's fancy
Like others, gone before.

We used to be so happy,
And could never wish for more,
Now our only link with Daddy
Is the postman at our door.

I see no great-coat hanging
With shiny buttons on,
I hear no voice calling
'Son, turn the radio on'.

Our home and hearts are empty
We miss the touch of his hand,
Each night, our prayers are all for Dad
To return from that other land.

I know other hearts are aching,
I'm sure they too feel sad,
And though mother's lonesome for her sweetheart
I'm just lonesome for my dad.

Anon

WHO WAS THE MAN?

Who was the man who invented the War?
Why did he do it and what was it for?
Ships on the ocean and ships in the air;
Silly old blighter, he ought to be there.

Who was the man who said, 'Parade stand at ease,
Carry on with inspection, Gentlemen please'.
Why should our buttons be shiny and bright,
Can anyone tell us what for we should fight?

I feel I cannot let you leave 21 Army Group on your
return to civil life without a message of thanks and
farewell. Together we have carried through one of
the most successful campaigns in history, and it has
been our good fortune to be members of this great team.
God Bless you and God speed.

B. L. Montgomery

FIELD MARSHAL
COMMANDER IN CHIEF

BAOR· 1945

Card sent to Captain Goodchild by Montgomery. (Courtesy of Northumberland
Hussars Museum)

People were starting to talk about what the world would be like after the war. The old certainties were being challenged with acid words on all sides of the argument. The author of 'Lonesome for My Dad' might be cynical about those who had sent the soldiers off to war but there were those who thought the alternatives a fearful thing. The election result of 1944 must have been a shock for those who had equated socialism with communism:

YOU'LL BE A SOCIALIST

If you can tell a falsehood without flinching,
And kid the British workman you're his friend
If you can legalise your ways of pinching,
The money that he's earned the right to spend.
If you can call your fellow creatures vermin
Because they live a decent, cultured life
And having preached against it, thus determine
Twixt class and class to foster social strife
If you can nationalize the source of fuel
And of it make a God Almighty mess
If you can make the public take its gruel
And kid them they've got more instead of less
If you can make our transatlantic cousins
Believe that, as a power you're still alive
That exports are increasing in their dozens
Although the six day week is now only five
If you can raise the price, and cut the vittles
And con the folks to work with all their will
And say, if someone your share belittles
'It's only Tory propaganda still'
If you can knock a ruddy empire sideways
And give it all away in one short year
If you can bust the whole exchequer wideways
And charge the overdraft to workers' beer
If you can go to functions in soft collars

If you can undervalue Britain's pound
If you can get tied up with Yankee dollars
Till no concise solution can be found.
If you can fill the unforgiving minute
With sixty seconds' grace of twist on twist
Then, the country's yours old cock and all that is in it
And, WHAT IS MORE, my son, YOU'LL BE A SOCIALIST!

Captain C. Funnell (Royal Military Police)

UNTITLED

It does no good to tell of how they died
Nor speak of 'heroes', glorifying War.
Let us rather be silent. Let our pride
Be that we knew these men who are no more.

Let us not say 'The King commissioned these'
List them within your memory as you please,
There is no rank distinction now for them.

March not in state; salute them not with guns;
They were not men for ceremonial show,
We shall remember: we shall tell their sons
In soldiers' words without Homeric flow.

Speak not of decorations, 'glorious ends',
Raise up no monuments with loud-voiced praises
Let us just simply say 'They were our Friends'
It is enough for we who knew those days.

J. Mead (107 Anti Tank Battery, Northumberland
Hussars, 1939–45)

Others were just plain glad it was all over at last:

VICTORY BELLS

Ring out the bells of joy o'er this fair land,
Let them go forth in golden, grateful mood,
And echo in the mountain solitude,
In crowded cities – on the ocean strand,
That is the day for which we prayed and planned.
And in the ending of the monstrous feud,
The present, past and future are renewed,
Let the world listen now and understand.

For peace and truth and love are come again
No longer threatened and no longer dim.
Since evil things lie shattered in the night,
Since wrong is trampled down by valiant right,
But in our joy let us give praise to him,
Without whose help all striving were in vain.

Adam Bury (*Newcastle Journal*, 9 May 1945)

THE SUN SHINES BRIGHTLY TODAY (extract)

The sun shines brightly down today
But on the horizon far away
Dark clouds gather with menace
An invading army waiting for the day

The cold winds of austerity are screaming
Through the land far and wide
Sweeping people along in their wake
Blowing away their hopes and their pride

But this has happened to us before
And people learnt to stand together
Marched to London with dignity and pride
Not looking for scapegoats forever

Tensions rise like unwanted weeds
Amongst the flowers of hope and love
Threats are uttered in voices
Where thought has been strangled at birth

Books are burned on the internet
So easy to forget the plaintive view
Of the man who said that where you burn books
You will later burn people too

Beware the false prophets who promise Utopia
Of the perfect future ahead
If we are just prepared to shed our humanity
On a road paved with the dead

If we fall again into the abyss
Allow the brave and the innocent to die
The voices of the future will accuse us
Echoing down the years: Why? Why? Why?

Peter Sagar

UNTITLED

If we should see the breadth of God
As wide as Heaven's span,
And measure by His magnitude
The littleness of man –
Our pettiness might die away,
Our dwarfing wrangles cease,
And man, with clearer eye, might walk
The shining fields of peace

Vivyen Bremner

SOURCES

Introduction

'The Poor Bloody Infantry' is quoted in Mallinson, A., *The Making of the British Army* (London, 2011) p. 480. 'Taint' is included courtesy of the Trustees of the Fusiliers Museum of Northumberland. 'Vale' is by kind permission of Joan Venables.

1 – 1939: *Sitzkrieg*

An extract from 'Marching Song of the 15/19 Hussars' together with 'And The Blue Around Their Caps' are reproduced by the kind consent of the Northumberland Hussars and 15/19 Hussars Archive (TWAM). 'Epitaph on a New Army' is from Selwyn, V., (ed.), *More Poems of the Second World War* (London, 1989) p. 39. The Cook correspondence appears courtesy of Durham County Record Office. McLuckie's poem is included by kind courtesy of the Trustees of the Fusiliers Museum of Northumberland. The poem by Hanns Pfeuffer is quoted in Hargreaves, R., *Blitzkrieg Unleashed* (Barnsley, 2008) p. 198. 'Heroes of the DLI' is reproduced by the kind permission of Durham County Record Office. 'Portsmouth Cypher School' is from *More Poems of the Second World War*, p. 26 and

'Entry 118' is also from *More Poems of the Second World War*, pp. 32–3. 'There was a Servant Girl' appears by the kind permission of the Trustees of the Northumberland Hussars and 15/19 Hussars Museum (TWAM).

2 – 1940: Blitzkreig

'Edgehill Fight', written for C.R.L. Fletcher's *A History of England* (1911), is quoted in Mallinson, p. 17. 'Untitled' thereafter is courtesy of the Fusiliers Museum of Northumberland. 'The Mantle' is from *More Poems*, p. 28. The extract from 'If the Invader Comes' is reproduced by the kind permission of Northumberland Record Office. 'Prisoner of War' appears courtesy of the Fusiliers Museum of Northumberland. 'Ode to the Home Guard', written 14 May 1943, and the quotation from the 'Home Guard Manual' is from the 2007 reprint. 'If', 'Tobruk Heroes' Dream', 'Heroic Tobruk', 'Australian Democracy', 'Mother & Son', and 'Old Tobruk' are included by the kind permission of the Trustees of the Fusiliers Museum of Northumberland.

3 – 1941: Standing Alone

The testimony of James Robert Ward is recorded as part of the Westall Project; http://www.northshields173.org (retrieved 8 February, 2013). 'Air Raid' is reproduced courtesy of The Northumberland Hussars and 15/19 Hussars Archive (TWAM). Jean Atkinson's letter is quoted with the kind permission of Anne Havis. 'The Party' is included courtesy of Rob Walker and www.warpoetry.com. 'Rare as Fairies' is quoted in MacDonald, C., *The Lost Battle: Crete 1941* (London, 1993) p. 148, 'The Paratroops Marching Song' is quoted in Sadler, J., *Operation Mercury* (Barnsley, 2007) p. 36, as is 'Ten Commandments of the Parachutist', p. 211. 'The Screaming Junkers' is from *The New Zealand Expeditionary Force Times*, 18 January 1943. 'Forward for New Zealand!' is quoted in Simpson, A., *Operation Mercury: The Battle for Crete* (London, 1981) pp. 254–5. 'Tribute to 50th Division' is reproduced by kind courtesy of the Northumberland Hussars and 15/19 Hussars

Archive. 'Fort Capuzzo' and 'Libyan Handicap' are included with the permission of the Trustees of the Fusiliers Museum of Northumberland.

4 – 1942: End of the Beginning

'Farewell to our Gallant Durhams' and 'My three strongest recollections' are from Durham County Record Office. 'Ode to Bully Beef' is quoted in Sadler, J., *Desert Rats* (Glos., 2012) p. 18. 'Code of the Desert Soldier' is quoted in Strawson, J., *The Battle for North Africa* (London, 1969) p. 8. 'Ode to a Desert Flower' is from *Crusader* vol. 57, 31 May 1943. The words of Private Lovell appear from *Listen to the Soldier*, courtesy of Durham County Record Office. 'El Alamein' is reproduced courtesy of Captain Sam Meadows 2 RGR. 'Eighth Army Hymn' is quoted in Sadler, J. *Desert Rats*, p. 244 as is 'Italian Marching Song' on pp. 224–5. 'Christmas at Agheila' is included with the kind permission of the Trustees of the Fusiliers Museum of Northumberland. 'Egyptian Fantasy' is reproduced courtesy of the Northumberland Hussars and 15/19 Hussars Archive (TWAM). 'Tank' is from *More Poems*, pp. 152–3. 'To be a Desert Rat' is from *Crusader* vol. 37, 11 January 1943.

5 – 1943: Beginning of the End

'Our Country' is reproduced with the kind permission of the Northumberland Hussars (TWAM). 'A POW's Meditation', 'To My Wife' and 'Bill the Bandsman' and 'Untitled' are included courtesy of the Trustees of the Fusiliers Museum of Northumberland, asis 'The Prisoner of War'. The Captain Goodchild correspondence is included courtesy of Northumberland Hussars (TWAM). 'The Tale of Transport' is included courtesy of Northumberland Records Office. 'The Scottish Girl's Lament' is courtesy of the Northumberland Hussars and 15/19 Hussars Archive (TWAM). 'D-Day Dodgers' is by kind permission of Mrs Margaret Ward. 'Parade Service on Deck', 'Beach Casualty', 'Italian Phrases', 'Salerno Fragment' and 'These Are Your Sons' are reproduced with the kind permission of Durham County Record Office. 'A Voyager's Song' is courtesy of G.F. Gallie and www.warpoetry.com. The untitled poem on p. 95 is reproduced courtesy of the Trustees of the Fusiliers Museum of Northumberland.

6 – 1944–45: The Second Front

'The Legend of Bill Millin' is included with the kind permission of Tony Church and www.warpoetry.com. Verse and prose by the late Maurice Pinkney are reproduced with kind permission of the Shepherd family and extracted from their private memoir *Maurice and Mary.* 'I will always remember my 21st Birthday' is with the kind permission of the Northumberland Hussars and 15/19 Hussars archive (TWAM). The story of the Fusiliers' drum is included with the kind permission of the Trustees of the Fusiliers Museum of Northumberland.

7 – Empire of the Sun

'Call of the West' is included with the kind permission of Durham County Record Office. 'Soldiers' is included with the kind permission of the Trustees of the Fusiliers Museum of Northumberland. 'Dead Japanese' is from *More Poems,* p. 309. Prose extract from 'Kohima' is from Arthur, M., *Forgotten Voices of the Second World War* (London, 2005) pp. 391–2. 'Wrap Up All My Care and Woe' is quoted in Fraser, G.M., *Quartered Safe Out Here* (London, 2003) p. 80. 'LIAP 22B' is courtesy of the Northumberland Hussars and 15/19 Hussars archive (TWAM).

8 – Aftermath

'Recessional' is quoted in Mallinson, p. 394. 'Aftermath' is from *More Poems,* p. 315. The collection of poems from 'I Want to go Home' and 'You'll be a Socialist' are reproduced by kind permission of the Trustees of the Fusiliers Museum of Northumberland. The poem by J. Mead is by kind consent of the Northumberland Hussars (TWAM). 'The Sun Shines Brightly Today' is quoted by kind permission of Peter Sagar and appears in *Tales from the Real World*, stories and poetry from the Thursday morning class at the Millin Centre, Benwell, Newcastle upon Tyne (Newcastle, 2012). 'Victory Bells' is included by kind permission of Northumberland Records Office. UNtitled poem by Vivyen Bremner from I Tune The Instrument (London, 1941)

Every endeavour has been made by the authors to trace copyright holders, and, where those in respect of all verse and extracts quoted herein and where those works have been previously published, their publishers. Copyright remains vested in the original holder. Where the authors have established the copyright of individuals and organisations, these have been listed in the acknowledgements together with permission to publish. The authors and publishers would be pleased to hear from anyone who feels they have been missed out and will undertake to amend the acknowledgements section accordingly in any future reprint.